BEWARE...

You are about to enter an ESCAPE BOOK. If you don't know what one of those is, then perhaps we should explain. An Escape Book is a form of puzzle book in which the unwary reader may become trapped for eternity. It is an escape room in the form of a book. You can decide on your own path, but your route is often controlled by the solutions you give to the puzzles you encounter along the way. You must solve the puzzles to escape the pages.

Some puzzles will offer you alternative routes according to your solution. Others will invite you to calculate the next entry you should turn to. When this happens, you should check the 'from' number to ensure that you came from the right location and are still on the right path. If you find that you have arrived from the wrong place, you should turn back and think again.

Not all wrong solutions will end the story. As befits an adventure in which you play the role of Sherlock Holmes, this book is far more cunning than that. Some wrong answers may have unforeseen consequences further down the path, causing you to miss a helpful clue or even land a red herring.

While you are trapped inside the Escape Book, you should pay attention to everything you see. Once the game is afoot, there are all manner of clues hidden on the pages. Use Watson's Notebook – which you will discover shortly – to record your observations. Some of these notes might be needed to solve later puzzles. You will also be required to master the Code Wheel, located on the cover of the book (of which, more later). If you are struggling with your art of deduction, you will find some helpful hints and clues (and even the answers) located at 221A and 221B, found at the back of the book.

There is more than one door through which you can exit the Escape Book. Some doors are marked with triumph... others with infamy. Only the most observant of detectives will find an escape route that results in newspaper headlines proclaiming their heroic success.

▶ *These arrows direct you to your next entry.*
Now, all great adventures begin by turning the first page...

WATSON'S NOTEBOOK

Use this notebook to jot down anything of interest you encounter during your adventure; you may find it helps you to solve a later puzzle.

NOTES & OBSERVATIONS

I brought along my Morse code notes.
(These can be found in entry 93.)

► *If you have yet to begin your adventure – Turn over the page*
(Feel free to refer to Watson's Notebook at any time.)

THE STORY

In the upcoming adventure, you will take on the role of the world's most famous consulting detective, Sherlock Holmes, as he becomes trapped within a dastardly plot. You will see everything from his point of view, you will attempt to solve the puzzles with his powers of deduction, you will be him! You might even find a magnifying glass helpful. So, try to think in the way that Sherlock thinks. As he once said, in Sir Arthur Conan Doyle's *The Sign of the Four* (1890): "When you have eliminated the impossible, whatever remains, HOWEVER IMPROBABLE, must be the truth."

You will be accompanied, of course, by your faithful companion Doctor John H. Watson. He will offer you words of advice, a voice of reason and a steady hand in times of peril. You should also make good use of his notebook to record observations that may help with your escape.

This adventure is set in a magnificent villa in Regent's Park, in central London, on an April afternoon and night in 1894. Doctor Watson has been in a subdued state, mourning his recently deceased wife Mary, and still recovering from the loss of his great friend Sherlock Holmes, whom he and all the world believes died following a titanic struggle with Professor Moriarty at the Reichenbach Falls in 1891. But Holmes has cheated death, and the events of this story play out on the very day after the great detective has stunned Watson by returning in disguise as a bookseller in order to outwit Moriarty's associate Colonel Sebastian Moran, and solve the celebrated *Adventure of the Empty House*.

Our story begins when Holmes receives a letter, apparently sent by the long-dead Charles Babbage, developer of the Analytical Engine in the 1860s and early 1870s. Today, the Engine is widely considered to be the world's first computer and the machine for which Babbage's associate Ada Lovelace wrote the earliest forerunner of modern computer algorithms. The letter invites Holmes and Doctor Watson to St Thomas's Lodge, Regent's Park, implying that they will see a transformed version of the Engine, which was never completed by Babbage or Lovelace. Meanwhile, Sherlock's brother Mycroft is missing. Could this be connected to the mysterious letter?

THE CODE WHEEL

Set into the cover of the Escape Book is a Code Wheel, which is an essential part of your equipment for solving some of the puzzles you will encounter. It features a series of windows behind which are letters, numbers, colours and a sequence of symbols. These can be used in a number of ways:

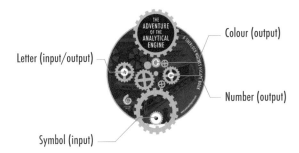

You can find a digital version of the Code Wheel at:
https://www.ammonitepress.com/gift/sherlock-analytical-engine-wheel/

In some puzzles you'll discover coded messages in the form of unintelligible notes or secret symbols hidden in the story. Using the Code Wheel, input your discoveries in the relevant *input* dial, then decode them by reading the relevant *output* dial.

To begin your adventure, you must first unlock the Escape Book. To do this, you should use the Code Wheel to solve the following cipher:

▶ *The secret code should reveal the time of day your adventure begins.*
Once you have solved the puzzle – Turn to 1

① BAKER STREET

"Here are this morning's letters, gentlemen," says Mrs Hudson, entering Sherlock's rooms at 221B Baker Street, "with some ham, boiled eggs, tea, toast, Dundee marmalade..." She stops, seeing an unfamiliar visitor.

"May I introduce my mother?" you ask. "Mrs Hudson, Mama; Mama, Mrs Hudson."

"Charmed, I'm sure," says Mrs Hudson, unloading the food onto the table.

"I always say, Mama, that Mrs Hudson has as good an idea of breakfast as a Scotchwoman."

"Yes, yes," says Mrs Holmes. "Rather late for breakfast, wouldn't you say? The morning has all but gone... Now, what on earth lies behind your sudden reappearance, Sherlock?"

After the infamous incident at the Reichenbach Falls of 1891, you have been travelling abroad, incognito, for three years.

"Just yesterday," Watson says, "he stunned me by reappearing in the guise of a bookseller..."

"I have been lying low, Mama, but had to return to solve the mysterious murder of the Honourable Ronald Adair... in an empty house..."

"I think I shall call it *The Adventure of the Empty House*," says Watson. "Which we solved last night by outwitting no less a figure than the redoubtable Colonel Sebastian Moran..."

"Thank goodness you're back to help find your dear brother, then," Mama says. "No one has heard from him since Tuesday March 27."

Watson spreads out his copy of the previous day's *Evening Gazette*.

> *The Gazette* understands that leading members of the Establishment have been invited to the unveiling of a Marvellous Engine in a Regent's Park villa on Saturday 7 April 1894.

"That's tomorrow," says Mrs Holmes. "And just a stone's throw from here."

"Thank you, Mama," you say, trying to contain your impatience with her for spelling everything out.

"I have been meaning to ask, sir," Mrs Hudson says, sounding agitated, "do you know what is making that awful rumbling noise in the middle of the night? I haven't slept a wink for a week."

You wonder as to the cause. Whatever is making the noise, you think, cannot be that far away.

Watson takes up the post. "Ah, good," he says, "some immediate action." He holds out a letter, marked 'Sherlock Holmes – Master Detective'.

"The news that I'm alive is spreading then," you say.

"Not necessarily, old chap... The postmark is 7 April 1870."

"Goodness gracious," says Mrs Hudson. "And it says, 'From the desk of Charles Babbage'."

▶ *You refuse to take the letter – Turn to 35*

▶ *You take the letter and examine it – Turn to 57*

② LIBRARY

Following the map, you trace your way down to the library. You see that two of its walls support bookcases that are seven feet tall; one wall contains a fireplace 53 inches across; and the fourth wall holds a window 48 inches tall, giving onto the garden.

There are three comfortable-looking armchairs arranged around a large sandy-red rug before the fireplace.

You sense the hidden hand sending you messages to direct you on a predetermined path through the lodge... What is the connection between Bertram Alfreds and this villa, and Charles Babbage? And the Order of the Silver Sun?

Watson interrupts your reverie. "What a beautiful room, Holmes..." he enthuses, "A truly splendid Afghan knotted rug."

You sit. You are tired. A few minutes' rest? How long have you been here?

But Watson interrupts you again. "Look, Holmes, there is something a little odd over here."

Standing beside him you see that a selection of books at eye level on one of the bookcases has been tampered with. Several are missing a single letter from their title. The librarian has either rubbed the letters off or covered them with small pieces of leather. You look at the books and an idea hits you.

"Note down the missing letters, Watson, and see if they make a message."

PARADISE LOST | BEOWULF | KIDNAPPED | BLEAK HOUSE | JANE EYRE | ON LIBERTY | VANITY FAIR | WUTHERING HEIGHTS | OEDIPUS REX | FRANKENSTEIN, OR THE MODERN PROMETHEUS | TESS OF THE D'URBERVILLES

▶ *If your message sends you to the fireplace –*
Turn to 24

▶ *If your message sends you to the window –*
Turn to 66

▶ *If your message sends you to the bookshelf on the opposing wall –*
Turn to 58

③ ENGRAVED BOX

On closer inspection, you find that the wooden box's delicate engravings are, in fact, words. You read aloud: "Follow the instructions to push a button, but know, only one of the four statements is true."

You examine the box. There are four buttons on the front; each button features a number.

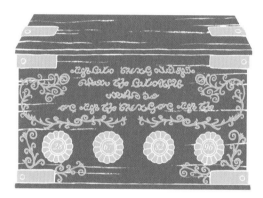

You gesture Watson over and read the four statements aloud:
"Push 28!
The right button to push is one of 28 and 96.
Don't push 96.
The right button to push is one of 67 and 82."

Watson looks a little confused. "Surely we just follow the instructions, Holmes? Push 28?"

"Possibly... Remember, though, Watson, only one of the statements is true. Perhaps a little more deduction is needed."

▶ *Find your answer and turn to it*

(4) BEDROOM

"To the Bedroom," Watson says, consulting the floor plan. You follow him downstairs to the second floor, back through the Chapel, across a short corridor, over the main upper landing, through another corridor and then through the heavy oak Bedroom door.

There is a musty smell and a layer of dust on the bedspread. No one has slept in the bed for a long time. There is, however, a fire burning in the hearth and, above it, a full kettle of water. The water is steaming hot, not yet boiled.

"Why do we keep walking into rooms that seem to have recently been abandoned?" Watson asks, rather peevishly. He picks up a letter. "Addressed to Mr Sudhakara Dvivedi," he says. The sheet inside is covered in a beautiful script. "Sanskrit, Holmes, how curious."

"Ah, Sudhakara Dvivedi – how splendid," you say. "I met Dvivedi in the Stranger's Room at the Diogenes Club, where I had been invited by Mycroft. Only room in the club where you're allowed to talk, you know. He is an Indian mathematician. His published works are all in Hindi and Sanskrit, and he was in London, and learning English. He had a very well-spoken friend – an interpreter, if you like. And we had the most stimulating conversation. I would venture..." you pause.

"What's that, Holmes?"

"I would venture that he is the most brilliant man I have ever met." Watson gazes at you.

"But what is not clear to me," you continue, "is how Mr Dvivedi is connected to this whole mystery? Why is this letter here? And what is the link between him, this Bertram Alfreds and the Babbage machine?"

"Look at this, Holmes." Watson has identified another puzzle.

▶ *Turn to 108*

⑤ CIGAR CABINET

You walk confidently to the cigar cabinet and examine the contents. Watson's eyes gleam with excitement, but you're a little less impressed. You're more of a pipe man, really.

The cabinet is unlocked. You pull the glass door towards you. There are shelves and shelves of rolled tobacco leaves. The smell is overwhelming.

You note a framed photograph propped up on the top shelf.

"By Jove," Watson says, turning to you quizzically. "I do believe that is Moriarty!"

You exhale gently. Watson is indeed correct. A picture of Moriarty, smirking, standing next to a man you don't recognize. How peculiar.

Your eyes scan the cabinet for any remaining clues and, finding nothing, you move on.

▶ *Inspect the desk – Turn to 88*

▶ *Investigate the engraved box – Turn to 3*

CARRIAGE 417

Carriage 417 pulls up next to you and the coachman hops down to open the door. He is a little shorter than expected, and as he pulls on the handle you note a few tendrils of silky hair resting on a rather slender neck.

"Watch out for the toolbox!" the coachman shouts as you climb in.

You watch your step and look closely at the floor, but there is nothing there. No toolbox in sight. How odd. The voice stirs something in your memory. You peer at the coachman, but he quickly turns away.

You settle yourself on one of the plush satin seats, noting the surprising floral scent and the several inches of mud caked on the coachman's boots.

"Where to?" the coachman asks.

"St Thomas's Lodge, Regent's Park," Watson pipes back. "I have a suspicion it was an unknown residence of the late Charles Babbage..." Watson is beaming from ear to ear. He has always had a fascination for strange engines. "...Creator of the Analytical Engine," he continues. "Never built of course, just designed, but a marvel all the same."

"I was always rather more interested in his collaborator Ada Lovelace," the coachman offers in response. "They worked together for several years, you know, and she even wrote some instructions for the Engine. Together, they developed a special method for referring to lines in an algorithm. It's a simple cipher, really. They used letters in the alphabet to represent numbers. So, a 'B' would indicate that you should consider line two; a 'G' would indicate you should consider line seven..."

What an odd thing for a coachman to say, you think, and rather impertinent. You say nothing, but the fact lodges itself in the back of your mind.

▶ *Turn to 98*

⑦ BIBLE MESSAGE – 'MORE'

You mark the final word and pick up the Bible.

"He made an engine. It will cause terror. Make it be no more," you read aloud.

You are both silent for a moment.

"Well, I don't know if I – it can't be that..." Watson splutters. He takes a deep breath. "Babbage's machine was never meant to cause terror, or harm of any kind," he says indignantly. "Can we trust this message? Maybe we've got something wrong."

"This is not, nor was it ever, the house of Charles Babbage," you reply. Again, you wonder at Watson's credulity and at how much your sudden return seems to have disturbed him.

"But he – or his work – is somehow at the heart of this adventure," you say.

Watson says nothing. He avoids your eye and walks quickly towards the door in frustration, but as he does so his foot catches on a floorboard and he stumbles slightly.

He attempts to hide his fuchsia face as you join him to investigate the scene beneath his feet.

There appears to be a word carved into the wood. Watson reads it aloud.

"That's straightforward enough," you say.

► *Turn to 29*

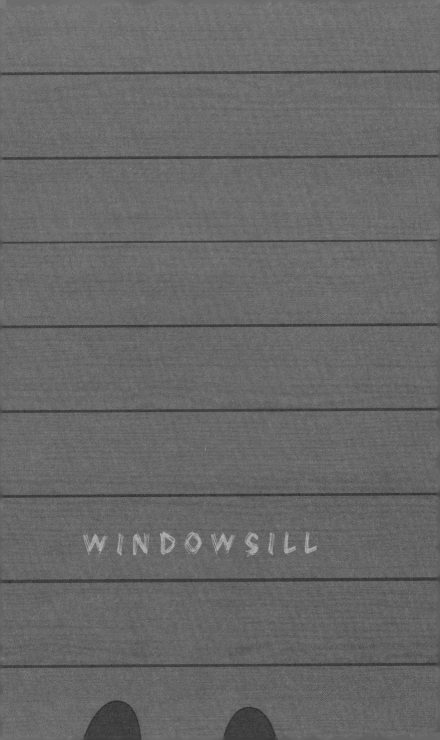

WINDOWSILL

SEARCHING FOR EIGHT

from 64

"Eight." What might the number mean?

"I'll have a look around to see if there is a group of eight objects anywhere in the room," Watson says, still breathing rather heavily.

You also scour the room.

"Aha." You spot two shelves together making the shape of a figure of eight. This is the right way to go...? But, you wonder, how has he hidden information here?

You walk over to the shelves. "The back. A mirror points to what is behind, or to the back," you say.

You gently remove the back of the shelves, and a letter falls out.

Watson looks at you in awe.

"Elementary, my dear Watson."

You both examine the letter.

"So, you are at the heart of this plan, Holmes..."

"Things are somewhat clearer, are they not?" you say.

"We must press on," Watson says breathlessly. "I suggest we make our way to the Ballroom."

► *Turn to 100*

Twenty-fourth day of July 1890

James Moriarty Esquire

James,

First, I must congratulate you that Holmes was heard calling you the Napoleon of Crime. But I must say that, for all that, you have never won a lasting victory over him, have you?

I received your reply to my letter about the Engine. How long ago it seems since we were not-so-happy schoolboys together. Then, as now, you missed no opportunity to assert your superiority over me. True, many teachers favoured you and you won many prizes, leaving me in second place...

While in my family, too, I was in second place – or lower, even. As you know, I could never win the love and approbation of my great uncle Charles Babbage – nor of the Countess Ada.

But I always knew I was more gifted than Babbage, than the Countess, than you. And with this machine I will prove my greatness. I will complete the Engine that Uncle Charles and the Countess could not. And I will better you by entrapping and humiliating the great Sherlock Holmes...

You will have to watch me become famous and celebrated. I will be remembered always as the Master of the Analytical Engine...

⑨ GLASS CUPBOARD

from 26

Through the yellow-panelled door there is... nothing. You sigh. The door opens to reveal a full-length cupboard full of glasses and decanters.

"We're wasting our time, Holmes..." Watson turns away at once.

But what's this? You observe some kind of crumpled, stained rag on the floor. "Did you miss this, old chap?" you say, holding up the rag. "Oil stains," you add, authoritatively.

Nevertheless, the yellow panel was evidently a mistake, and you reconsider your options.

▶ *Turn to 26*

⑩ MAIN DRAWING ROOM

from 37

Entering the Main Drawing Room, you see that tea has been laid out on a small table beside the fireplace.

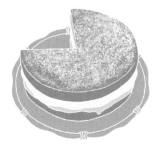

This does not fill you with joy. What you would like is a few moments alone with your violin, a few moments for thinking, a chance to escape Watson's incessant chatter – not to have to listen to the sounds of him slurping tea and chomping on more food.

"Look at this, Holmes," Watson says. "There is a pot, a milk jug, two china teacups and saucers, two small plates and a round cake. But a piece is missing from the cake."

"I, too, have eyes, Watson."

You scan the room. A grandfather clock, not working – the hands point to roughly 1:12 – and a small door beside it leading to... what? A cupboard?

Three armchairs.

The cake could be another message, you think. The door interests you. You try it and find it is locked.

Watson is busy helping himself to tea. "Could you spare a moment, Watson, to look for a key to fit this door?" You try the wooden compartment beneath the clock face on the grandfather clock. Locked, or jammed... it won't open.

A thorough search of the room yields nothing.

You think again. Something to do with the shape of the cake intrigues you. Can you recreate the shape in any other part of the room?

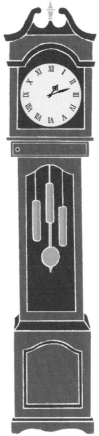

▶ *You recreate the shape – Turn to 44*

▶ *You are unable to recreate the shape – Turn to 33*

A HUMILIATING RESCUE

from 25, 95

Nothing happens. You look around rather sheepishly at the others.

Mycroft pulls out his pocket watch. "Well," he says, "the unveiling of the Analytical Engine is due to start shortly. Looks like you are going to be Alfreds' prize exhibit, Sherlock... Death defeated."

"Surely we can explain the truth of the situation," says Dvivedi, in a rather doubtful tone.

"I'm not sure anyone will take our word over Alfreds'," says the Archbishop, "since we are here in his machine."

A clattering of the machine opening. You grit your teeth and prepare for the worst.

But you are surprised. "Mama!" You and Mycroft exclaim in unison.

"Good morning, Archbishop, Mr Dvivedi, Doctor Watson," she says, pointedly ignoring you and your irritating brother.

"What has happened? What about the Great Unveiling of the Marvellous Engine?"

"My darlings, I read the papers we were looking at in Baker Street about the Engine and, putting two and two together, found some background information of my own. And I was helped with one or two key details by a very helpful coachman who called around with a glove he said you left in his carriage. A very fetching coachman, I must say...

"So, I made my way here and was able to unmask that charlatan Alfreds before he made his demonstration of the machine and signed the government contract he had lined up."

"Well, the plan is at least foiled," says Dvivedi.

"Thank the good Lord," the Archbishop adds.

"I have the personal thanks of the Prime Minister, who was in attendance. All is settled. But I'm very disappointed in you, my boys. Perhaps you lost your touch during your long absence, Sherlock."

► *Turn to 97*

⑫ GREY DOOR

from 31

You pick the grey door and are halfway across the room to try it when Watson rather irritatingly says, "I think not, Holmes."

You look back at him. He is at least not grinning at you, but instead looking at the picture of the Flying Scotchman and stroking his chin.

You decide to choose again.

► *Turn to 31*

(13) CHAPEL

As the door swings open, Watson steps nervously into what appears to be a chapel.

There is a small altar at the far end beneath a stained-glass window of Jesus walking on water. There is very little daylight coming through the window; you judge there must be trees outside. As in the Trophy Room, there are several portraits, propped up against the altar and on the floor, each with a candle burning before it.

Here and there you see cards displaying the words, 'The Order of the Silver Sun'.

My, my, what an extraordinary place. You note that the portraits are all of the same man. A shrine to Babbage.

In the gloom you both see something glinting.

Manuscript books have been left open on tables. You do your best to read the spidery handwriting by the low-level daylight and candlelight.

"Holmes! Holmes! Holmes!"

Watson is in a gloomy corner by the glinting object. It looks like a cog or some other machine part.

"Look, Holmes, it's levitating by some ghostly power. What confounded trickery is this?"

"I think not," you say. It's true that there is nothing supporting the machine part that is several feet off the ground, but Watson has not noticed the slender cord suspending it from the ceiling. You pull the cord and make the cog fly towards you.

> My Analytical Engine is a vast improvement on my Difference Engine. It can perform generalized operations, where the DE can only perform calculations... My design includes an internal chamber housing key controls, including an off switch. The internal chamber is high security and cannot be exited while the machine is in use. It is large enough to contain four people as calculators.

"Ah, Holmes, I – I see..."

In the far corner of the room, a door has been propped open, giving onto a narrow staircase.

▶ *Turn to 50*

STRAIGHT AHEAD

"I think we just need to go straight ahead," you say, turning to Watson.

"To the front door?" Watson asks.

"Indeed," you say.

You walk to the front door. You push, pull, and try to turn the handle. Nothing moves.

"I don't think that can be right, Holmes," Watson calls. "Let's take another look at these engravings."

"I'm going to have to agree with you," you answer gloomily. "Although I'm a little relieved. It would have been rather frustrating to have found out the front door was in fact open all this time."

You join Watson on the stairs to take another look at the puzzle.

▶ *Turn to 93*

BILLIARD BALL '19'

You reach for the ball, but Watson stops you.

"I don't think the colour can be correct, Holmes," he says, gesturing to the fourth chalked triangle. "There is already one yellow, one green and one red. I think perhaps the ball we're looking for is blue."

You let your hand fall to your side. Watson does seem to be correct.

Through gritted teeth, you say, "Let's take another look, then," and return to the billiard ball sequence.

▶ *Turn to 41*

TILE 16

The tile comes off the roof with surprising ease.

You weigh it in your hands, then hold it up in front of you to inspect the handwriting.

"Holmes," Watson says, "look at the sequence of numbers on the back here."

You turn the tile over to find a short message and a sequence of numbers. The message reads:

Ready for a rest? A spin will get you there.
6 / 2 / 10 / 19 / 16 / 16 / 26

"A spin?" you muse aloud. Watson is already reaching into his coat pocket for the Code Wheel to help decode the message.

▶ *Consult the floor plan – Turn to the number you discover*

TO THE LINEN CUPBOARD?

from 79

"17," you say. "What does that mean?"

Watson shrugs. He turns the paper over. "Aha," he says, then reads: "To find out where to go next add twice 13."

"43," you say at once.

Watson consults the floor plan. "To the linen cupboard?" he asks.

As you approach the door Watson trips and falls. His feet are entangled in one of the sheets. He writhes for a moment, but you are altogether too distracted by what he has uncovered to notice. It's a large metal safe. A gold geometric design surrounds a complex combination lock. You cast your eye around the room to the other covered pieces of furniture.

"Should we go to the linen cupboard, or stay and investigate?" Watson asks.

▶ *Stay and investigate – Turn to 61*

▶ *Go straight to the linen cupboard – Turn to 43*

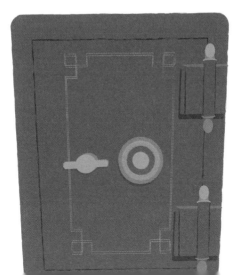

"T, R, A, P," Watson repeats.

You are already at the trapdoor, opening it. You find some wooden steps leading down into some kind of storage area, lit with candles.

"Extraordinary," breathes Watson. "Someone has been here recently, perhaps they remain with us now..." He begins to tiptoe about the room.

You exhale deeply. "He wants us to feel as though we're chasing a ghost."

"Yes," Watson replies. "And could it be that his machine really does work?"

You don't respond. It's all too much of a performance, you think. A man reaching for something and falling short.

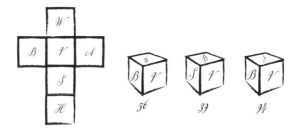

"Look," Watson says, pointing. "Another puzzle?" On the wall is a sketch of a flattened cube with six letters, and on the other three walls are different configurations of the cube, each labelled with a number.

"We must have to work out which of the three cubes it is possible to make from the net."

You look at the cubes and make your choice.

▶ *Turn to the number you discover*

"HE TRICKED US ALL"

"He tricked us all," the Archbishop interjects. "He invited Mr Dvivedi to visit the world's most powerful mathematical device; told Mycroft that the machine could be a marvellous tool for the government; and told me that the Engine allowed him to speak directly to God."

"And the event?" you ask.

Dvivedi responds. "Well, it's all under the guise of this Order of his. The Order of the Silver Sun will bring your loved ones back from the dead, and this machine is how they claim they'll do it, for just a few thousand pounds."

"You know Alfreds was thrown out of the Hermetic Order of the Golden Dawn?" Mycroft asks. "I believe that is why he is so fixated on the veil and the 'other side'. His Order is an attempt to prove himself better."

"The big public launch is today at nine o'clock," Mycroft says. "And I imagine it'll be packed to the rafters, Saturday or no Saturday. Endless possibilities – a never-ending military, an always replenishing workforce..."

"He could claim to be able to bring back St Paul, or even Our Lord Himself," says the Archbishop.

"Or use it as a threat," muses Dvivedi, "to bring back the demon Kabhanda from our mythology, or Genghis Khan, or Napoleon..."

"It's a very expensive con," Mycroft says.

"And not just financially," says the Archbishop. "It is a horrendously cruel thing to suggest you can bring back a loved one when in fact you cannot."

"But I imagine that's why you're here, Sherlock." Mycroft jumps in. "Because you're supposed to be dead, aren't you?"

▶ *Turn to 80*

TROPHY ROOM

You enter the room ahead of Watson. There are eight portraits on the wall in front of you. Your keen eye assesses them: they are all of the same person at different ages, from a young buck to an older man aged around 70 or so.

You take your bearings. On the right-hand wall is a trophy cabinet; on the left, a gun case and a stuffed stag's head; on the floor there is a lion's skin, complete with head. Ugh, a sportsman.

It is a large space and well-lit through a substantial window giving onto another garden view. Closed. And locked. The sun is shining outside. Late-afternoon sunlight, you judge. April in London, you think. Sunset would be around 6:45pm or so. You wonder what the time is. Your pocket watch is back at Baker Street, still in pieces while you attempt to repair it after it was damaged on your travels in Tibet and Persia.

In the trophy cabinet, you find a bent, rolled-up certificate. It looks as if someone has tried to hide it hurriedly. It is in the name of Bertram Alfreds, for second prize in mathematics, behind a certain… James Moriarty. You spot a framed photograph of Moriarty standing next to a man you don't recognize. Well, well. You feel you are beginning to get an inkling of what is going on but can't quite put your finger on it.

Watson is pointing at the portraits. "Take a look here, and here. And here." He does like to state the obvious.

"Symbols, Watson. No doubt a coded message."

Watson takes out the Code Wheel to translate the symbols to letters.

▶ *Go to the gun case – Turn to 34*

▶ *Go to the trophy cabinet – Turn to 77*

▶ *Go to the stag's head – Turn to 45*

LOOKING FOR A CAB

Watson scurries down the stairs ahead of you. His tweed is heavy and you had to bunch the trousers he gave you at your waist and hold them up with a thick belt. You can tell that, like you, he is thrilled to be solving cases once again. The Ronald Adair murder and the efficient capture of Colonel Moran last night was... a joy.

Together, you emerge onto the street. Watson has removed the envelope to check the instructions and your eyes catch something on the back.

"Wait a second, old chap," you say to him, "turn that over."

On the back of the envelope is another message. It's written in a different hand to the note, and not one you recognize. Or... perhaps... You brush the thought away.

You examine the message closely. There are four statements, three numbers and one muddy smudge.

Watson reads the message aloud and then beams at you. He'd never admit it, but he's missed this. You can tell.

You observe the street. Hansom cabs are passing, clattering over the cobblestones, each one with a three-digit number emblazoned on the side. You watch closely, allowing the statements and the numbers to mix in your mind.

► *Hail Carriage 741 – Turn to 70*

► *Hail Carriage 147 – Turn to 85*

► *Hail Carriage 417 – Turn to 6*

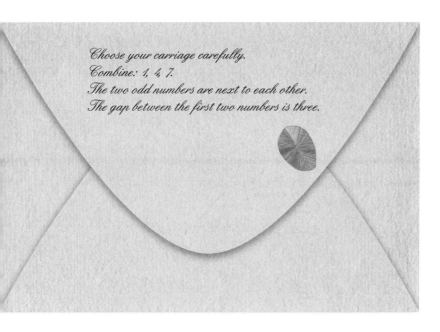

Choose your carriage carefully.
Combine: 1, 4, 7.
The two odd numbers are next to each other.
The gap between the first two numbers is three.

INSIDE THE SAFE

The safe swings open. Watson looks elated.

He reaches in and pulls out several long scrolls of paper. Together, you spread these flat on the floor.

The first is a handwritten document with the title 'The Order of the Silver Sun'. The second is a sketch of a large engine – a huge oblong shape with cogs, wheels, pulleys, and what you can only describe as wings.

Watson considers the document, scratching his head. "Through the veil?" he asks.

"Yes," you nod. "It appears Alfreds has some claim to returning people from the afterlife."

"A highway between the land of the living and the land of the dead. The one you trod, Holmes."

Is he joking? you wonder. "Watson, old chum..." you begin.

He isn't listening, and instead is engrossed in the sketches of the Engine. "Holmes! These look almost identical to the diagrams of Babbage's machines, but this," he points to a large rectangle sketched halfway down the engine, "is definitely new."

You consider the diagram. The large rectangle is labelled 'the veil'.

Watson's eyes sparkle and he splutters as his brain launches into gear. "Perhaps – perhaps – someone built the engine, this Alfreds fellow, and then it brought Babbage back from the dead? Or maybe Babbage brought himself back? And the Order is –"

You need to find a way to put on the brakes.

The Order of the Silver Sun
established by Bertram Alfreds, 1892

For men who long for a life that transcends the veil.
Those who know the truth of the Silver Sun know
what it is to travel between the land of the living
and the land of the dead.

The Order's Engine opens a doorway between the
worlds and allows those who have passed to rejoin
us. A séance on soil.

Watson – today, at any rate – is not the Watson of old. He is not himself.
You lay a hand on Watson's shoulder. He stops.

"You were always going to be able to use Alfreds' proof to prove Alfreds'
story," you say. "There is no one in this house but us and him, and the
Engine – which we need to find and stop."

You stand up.

► *Go to the linen cupboard – Turn to 43*

FORTY WINKS

Left. You look for doors on the left.

"That door there," Watson says.

You investigate. "Not this one, Watson. This gives onto the Smoking Room, where we have already been."

"But there aren't any others doors to the left."

"There might be – why don't we look through this archway?"

Sure enough you find a doorway just beyond the archway and enter a small drawing room. It is comfortable-looking, though there are newspaper pages strewn across the large rug. You are feeling exhausted and note the two deep armchairs and, on a table, a small plate of sandwiches and a decanter with two glasses. Perhaps a moment's rest, you think, and a little pick-me-up? You've been here for hours, to be sure. You can see only the depths of the April night outside.

Watson appears to be of the same mind. He slumps into one of the armchairs and lets out a long sigh. "Five minutes, Holmes?" he asks.

You both take a seat and Watson pours you each a drink.

"A very fine sherry," Watson says. He takes several sandwiches. How long has it been since Mrs Hudson's very fine breakfast, you wonder?

Your eyelids droop. You are distantly aware of Watson breathing gently.

Sometime later, you awake, feeling a little groggy. Watson is talking to you.

▶ *Turn to 75*

㉔ LIBRARY FIREPLACE

Watson saunters over to the fireplace. He crouches down and begins to sift through the ashy embers. You're not quite sure what he's looking for, and you're convinced that if you asked him, he wouldn't be sure, either.

You turn back to the bookshelf. Your eye is caught by Robert Louis Stevenson's *Kidnapped*, and its missing 'K'. There is no way the fireplace can be correct.

You call Watson back and together you return to the book spines.

▶ *Turn to 2*

㉕ YELLOW HANDLE

"Yellow," you say.

"Let's take our time, Mr Holmes," the Archbishop says. "Shall I say a prayer before you make your choice?"

You are sure. You turn the yellow handle. Nothing happens. Nothing.

The Archbishop clears his throat rather pointedly.

▶ *Turn to 11*

DINING ROOM

You lead the way into the Dining Room. On the large central table, five place settings have been laid with name-cards, candles and the finest linen. The cards read: Sherlock Holmes; Dr John Watson; The Ghost of Professor Moriarty; Your Host, Charles Babbage; and The Archbishop of Canterbury.

At the far end of the room are three doors, each with a brightly painted central panel: one blue, one green and one yellow. Curious. On the table, there are cut-glass wine glasses and five rather dusty wine bottles: Meursault Charmes, Château Lafite, Château Latour, Montrachet and Château d'Yquem. Hmm, very fine wines, you think.

Watson appears to be intrigued by the dates. "1846. 1865. 1870. They could all have been offered to us by Charles Babbage as our host..."

A long silence. "Please don't tell me you believe we're following his ghost?" you say, rolling your eyes.

Watson quotes *Hamlet*: "'There are more things in heaven and earth, Horatio, Than are dreamt of in your philosophy.'"

"Come along. You are a man of science. You have no time for ghosts..."

"I confess to feeling shaken, Holmes. Your sudden appearance yesterday seemed like you yourself could be a ghost, an adventurer returning from the land of the dead."

You snort. "Look at these tasting notes for Meursault," you say, noticing that various letters are in bold.

Colour? The doors at the far end are unusual... Would a gentleman have such bright colours in a dining room?

Watson is brandishing the Code Wheel. "I suggest..." he begins.

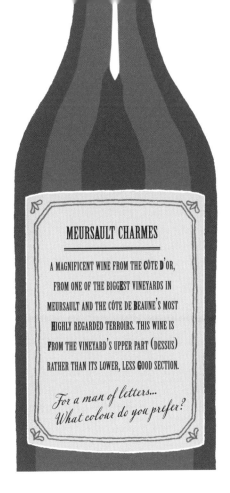

MEURSAULT CHARMES

A MAGNIFICENT WINE FROM THE CÔTE D'OR, FROM ONE OF THE BIGGEST VINEYARDS IN MEURSAULT AND THE CÔTE DE BEAUNE'S MOST HIGHLY REGARDED TERROIRS. THIS WINE IS FROM THE VINEYARD'S UPPER PART (DESSUS) RATHER THAN ITS LOWER, LESS GOOD SECTION.

For a man of letters...
What colour do you prefer?

He suggests! You're well ahead of him. You use the Code Wheel to establish what quality all the bold letters share.

► *Choose the yellow door – Turn to 9*

► *Choose the blue door – Turn to 53*

► *Choose the green door – Turn to 41*

DOWN THE TROPHY ROOM STAIRCASE

from 31

You can see a glimmer of light downstairs and decide to go down.

"Are you sure, old man?" Watson says, hesitating on the landing.

Down 11 steps of a spiral staircase you find the light is coming through a slatted door, rather like a fence or a gate. Looking through the slats you can see several plants, some French windows that give onto a garden, a tiled floor, a round table and some chairs – and what looks like a small staircase going down into the floor in the far corner.

It seems to be a garden room or conservatory of some sort. The scene is brightly lit by sunshine from the garden.

You begin to look around for some way of opening the door but can't find anything. You decide to retrace your steps.

Turning around and beginning to climb, you encounter Watson belatedly coming down. You indicate by a circular movement of your right index finger that he should turn around and head back.

▶ *Turn to 34*

BUTTON 28

Watson shakes his head. "I disagree, Holmes. I think that it really is that simple."

Perhaps he is correct? You pick up the box and prepare to push Button 28, but something stops you.

"If only one of the statements is true," you say aloud, "then that means all the others must be false. I don't believe 28 can be the correct button, Watson."

You put the box back on the table and return to the statements.

▶ *Turn to 3*

ATTIC WINDOWSILL

from 7, 42, 73

Watson follows sheepishly as you cross the room in just a couple of strides. You peer out of the window. The gardener is moving plants in the manicured garden below. The sun is sinking, and the sky is turning a deep pink, not dissimilar to the colour of Watson's cheeks.

Time is moving swiftly you observe, and you feel no closer to understanding who has really brought you here, or why.

You rest your hand on the windowsill and lean a little further out. You are surprised to feel a number of rough grooves beneath your fingertips.

Carved into the wood is another message: 'There is an extra tile here. Remove it.'

On the slope of the roof you spot a number of tiles in a visual sequence of sorts.

You're a little taken aback by the scale and number of these puzzles. Whoever has sent you on this journey evidently has a great deal of money and time at their disposal.

Watson peers behind your shoulder. "We need to remove the extra tile?" he asks.

"Yes. The tile that doesn't belong to the sequence," you respond.

You consider the scene for a few minutes, and then reach out the window to prise the extra tile from its position.

▶ *Turn to the number you discover*

(30)

'S'

from 43

"'S'," you say. "Look, it leads through to the centre."

Watson is holding the floor plan. "'S' leads us to the Scullery," he says. "Come on," he says, and hurries off.

You're not sure this feels right. From cupboard to Scullery? Should you call him back and reconsider?

▶ *If you think you should reconsider – Turn to 43*

▶ *If you think you should head to the Scullery – Turn to 91*

The answer leads you back to the Hall. A staircase climbs to a landing with two doors – one blue, one green – and at the foot is the grey door you noticed before. There are several portraits, but also some paintings of trains.

"Splendid picture of the Flying Scotchman," Watson murmurs. "1891."

There are two red rugs and a trapdoor. A corridor leads to a pink door. Curious that so many doors in the villa are brightly painted, you think.

A suit of armour has been manipulated into a contorted position: one foot raised and pointing, the left arm out at right angles, and the right arm pointing down. There is a document poking out of the visor. It reads: 'Look for a _ _ _ _ door. But first, combine LH, RH, RF, LF.'

"Look at this, Holmes!"

On the table, there are sticks of rhubarb. The suit of armour's right foot seems to be pointing to an apple, and by the left foot is a pear. Haven't you seen armour and fruit before?

Hmm, four missing letters, you think. So, the green door can be discounted. The answer must be connected to the pose of the suit of armour. Could the letters stand for left hand, right hand, right foot and left foot?

You set about trying to solve the puzzle.

▶ *Choose the blue door – Turn to 62*

▶ *Choose the grey door – Turn to 12*

▶ *Choose the trapdoor – Turn to 18*

▶ *Choose the pink door – Turn to 86*

TOWARDS THE SCULLERY

You make a move towards the door. Watson stands still.

"Holmes, are you sure? I believe we might be close. I'm not sure now is the time to be turning back."

You pause. Perhaps you misread the note? Or wrote a letter down wrong?

"I think we should take another look."

▶ *Return to the message – Turn to 68*

▶ *Go to the window – Turn to 92*

▶ *Go to the staircase – Turn to 78*

▶ *Proceed to the Scullery – Turn to 91*

STUMPED

"I'm a little stuck," you say, turning to Watson. "Any ideas?"

"Is there something else in the room that has a similar shape to this cake?"

You look around the room. Odd that the clock isn't working, you think.

"If not, perhaps we could go across to the Scullery? The cook might help us?"

▶ *If you can see a way to recreate the shape – Turn to 44*

▶ *Go to the Scullery – Turn to 91*

GUN CASE

The clues seem to lead to the gun case. It is rather a strange shape, you think – very tall and holding just two shotguns. And as you get closer you realize it is, in fact, a door.

At once you identify the hidden handle and open the door. Watson rushes over to catch up and tries to get past you and through the opening.

"Hold on," you say. Eagle-eyed as ever, you have noticed that on the back of the door is a sign hanging from one nail, as though someone has tried to remove it but hasn't had time to complete the task. It says: Bertram Alfreds, Esquire.

Aha, you think. You step back into the room and, from the trophy cabinet, take out one of the portraits of the two men. You look at their faces.

"This is our host," you say, pointing to the figure next to Moriarty.

"What?" Watson murmurs, vaguely.

"Oh, never mind," you say, and push past him through the doorway.

"I say, what?" he says to your back.

You are standing on a small landing, with stairs going up to the right and down to the left.

▶ *Go up the stairs – Turn to 107*

▶ *Go down the stairs – Turn to 27*

STAY IN HIDING?

"No, Watson, after yesterday's events only Lestrade, his two constables, yourself, Mrs H. and Mycroft know I am alive. Plus Colonel Moran. And now Mama. There may be some benefits from staying out of the public eye – I still have enemies, you know. Send the letter back unopened."

"But, the postmark…" says Mrs Holmes. "How can you not be interested?"

It's obviously irresistible. You are just playing with them.

"Perhaps I have developed a taste for going unnoticed." you say. "I achieved a good deal as the Norwegian Sigerson on my travels…"

You think of Mycroft and all he did to facilitate your return: keeping your rooms and preparing Mrs H. to perform the trick that foiled Moran…

"Come, Sherlock," says Mrs Holmes, waving the envelope under your nose.

► *You take the letter – Turn to 57*

BILLIARD BALL 'Z'

You reach for the ball but Watson stops you.

"I don't think that can be correct, Holmes," he says. "There is already one yellow, one green and one red. I think the ball we're looking for is blue."

You let your hand fall to your side. Watson does seem to be correct.

Through gritted teeth you say, "Let's take another look, then."

► *Turn to 41*

A CONNECTION TO MYCROFT?

Watson consults the floor plan. "Look here, old chap," he says, holding the floor plan out and gesturing to it. "There is a box here with an addition sign inside."

"We counted 37 squares... so, we're to add 3 and 7?" you ask. "Where is Room 10?"

"The Main Drawing Room," Watson responds. "Just next door."

As you turn to approach, your eye is caught by something on a low side table.

It is a newspaper from March 23, and stamped in the bottom left-hand corner is the insignia of the Diogenes Club. Watson is standing close behind you.

"Your brother Mycroft's club, Holmes," he says helpfully, once again stating nothing but the obvious.

Sticking out of the newspaper is a business card. It is blank on one side, but on the other you see the name of your brother. 'Mycroft G. Holmes' is printed at the top and there is a handwritten note below. It reads: 'Good to meet you today, B. I'm curious to see this contraption of yours. I'll pop by the house Tuesday next. Holmes.'

You run the newspaper's date and the handwritten note through your memory. "Mama said no one had seen Mycroft since Tuesday 27. Of last month. The Tuesday referenced here," you muse aloud.

"You don't think...?" Watson asks.

"I don't know." you respond. "Let's get on."

▶ *Turn to 10*

GARDEN SYMMETRY – FOUR MISSING

"Four are missing, in my view," you say.

"Are you sure, Holmes?" Watson says. "I'm not convinced."

You think again and return to the puzzle.

► *Turn to 66*

CUBE 39

"I think the cube with 39 is correct," you say and begin to climb out of the trapdoor.

But a doubt strikes as you do so. Turning back to Watson, you say, "In fact, I'm not sure that one's possible."

You both look again.

► *Turn to 18*

TRIUMPH

After a rather long-winded speech, Alfreds announces: "Lord Rosebery, gentlemen and ladies, in this truly historic moment I will demonstrate the power of my Analytical Engine to defeat Death itself. The money paid by the government will seem nothing when the consequences of the development become apparent."

There is a grinding of gears.

You hear: "I present to you the eminent detective Mr Sherlock Holmes, summoned from the dead by the power of this marvellous machine. In his company you will see the Most Reverend and Right Honourable Archbishop of Canterbury, who will vouch for the machine's power, the eminent Indian mathematician Sudhakara Dvivedi, who will vouch for its mechanical excellence…"

His voice trails away. There is laughter.

"An empty chamber! You're wasting our time!" You recognize the voice of the Prime Minister.

"This machine is nothing but a sham and a con!" That voice you know to be Craig Methven, chief reporter for *The Evening Gazette*.

Now you lead Sudhakara Dvivedi, the Archbishop, dear old Watson and (unavoidably, regrettably) the smirking Mycroft into full view.

"You are a charlatan, Mr Alfreds," you say. "Gentlemen, I have been in hiding these past three years, since the events at the Reichenbach Falls in '91. I survived the fight with Professor James Moriarty there and have travelled in Tibet, Persia and elsewhere.

"Alfreds believed that he could trick me into somehow proving the worth of his machine. But the entire enterprise is a scandal. He has been stealing money from the bereaved in the pretence that he can bring the dead back to life… He is a second-class inventor, a second-class mathematician and a poor excuse for an Englishman… I am delighted that I have been able to unmask him and save the country a great fortune."

"We, Holmes," Watson says. "We."

▶ *Turn to 87*

(41) BILLIARD ROOM

You take the green door and enter a candlelit room. In the centre of a plush carpet sits a billiard table. The balls are strewn across the baize. A cue is propped against one leg. A glass lies on its side on a small table.

"It's as if someone left suddenly," Watson says, "running for their lives. Or they want to stay hidden... Charles Babbage, for instance?" He shivers.

"He died in 1871, Watson."

"Everyone thinks he is dead, but I thought – everyone thought – you were dead, also. Perhaps he is only dead in the way you were dead."

You remind yourself that Watson is still grieving the loss of his wife. And the fact that, just yesterday, he had been shocked enough by your return to faint. He was out cold for an impressive length of time. You wonder how honest he'll be about that in his write up.

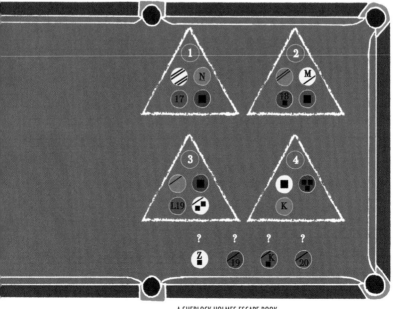

You turn your attention to the billiard table. As you move closer, it appears there is some logic to the balls' placement.

Watson reaches to pick up one of the balls, but you stop him. "I rather believe there is a different type of game afoot," you say.

Watson considers the scene aloud. "Aha! We need to select one of these balls here to complete the puzzle," he says, gesturing to a row of single billiard balls sitting directly ahead of him.

"Correct," you say. "We need to choose a ball that agrees with the sequence given, although I can't clearly see what it is yet..."

▶ *To select the 'Z' ball – Turn to 36*

▶ *To select the '19' ball – Turn to 15*

▶ *To select the 'K' ball – Turn to 83*

▶ *To select the '20' ball – Turn to 46*

(42) TILE 42

from 29

You prepare to reach for Tile 42. It's a good distance from the windowsill and you tap Watson's shoulder to ask him to move out of your way. As he does so, your eyes fall on the tile sequence again. From this new angle, Tile 42 no longer feels like the sensible option it once did.

You run through the sequence in your head, considering which tiles are added to the design as you move from one pattern to the next. You note your mistake and return to your position at the windowsill.

▶ *Turn to 29*

(ARIADNE IN THE) LINEN CUPBOARD

You move on to the linen cupboard.

As you look inside, your mouth drops open in surprise. The cupboard is large – the size of a small room – and is filled with strands of thin white thread. Long strings of thread reach from floor to ceiling, and from corner to corner, as though the room has been invaded by a mischievous insect and every single sheet has been pulled apart, thread by thread, to make a maze.

Through this network runs one red string. "Ariadne," you whisper.

"Yes, with a thread she enabled Theseus to escape the labyrinth after killing the Minotaur," Watson says. Who is he talking to? "So, I imagine we should follow the red thread... to escape... our predicament..."

As usual you are well ahead of him, but you have to pick your way slowly across the room because of the mass of white threads.

The red string leads to a maze drawn on the floor in red chalk. There seem to be three entrances, each with a letter – 'S', 'D' and 'Z'. You quickly see that you need to find the route that leads to the centre of the maze and then use the letter associated with that route to determine which room you should go to next.

► *If you think you should start at 'S' – Turn to 30*

► *If you think you should start at 'D' – Turn to 89*

► *If you think you should start at 'Z' – Turn to 93*

CAKE TIME

from 110.33

You deduce that the shape of the cake is meant to represent a time: quarter to 12.

You move the hands of the grandfather clock to that position and the compartment beneath the clock face springs open – revealing a key. You try the key in the wooden door and it opens ...

You poke your head through and look up and down. "It's a corridor Watson," you call out.

One minute, Holmes," he says. "Let me taste this cake! I – we – have hardly had a bite to eat since Mrs Hudson's breakfast and how many hours ago was that?"

You don't feel hungry. Once you get your teeth into a case, you feed on the intellectual challenge...

"It's delicious, old man. Lemon cake! Aren't you hungry?"

Lemon cake. Mama's favourite.

"Not a bit. And please hurry, Watson – let's get a move on!"

You clamber through the door and walk along the corridor. Watson follows.

"Light! Watson!" you exclaim. Watson fumbles in his pocket to pull out the matches and then strikes a feeble flame.

You find yourself in front of another small wooden door built into the wall. You push it open.

▶ Turn to 81

THE ADVENTURE OF THE ANALYTICAL ENGINE

STAG'S HEAD

The clues seem to lead to the stag's head.

What next? You look closely at the animal's head for a clue or lead, examining the fur, the teeth, the glassy eyes, the texture of the antlers.

Where is the stag looking? Is that a clue? Is there anything hidden around or behind it? You try to remove it from the wall. No luck.

"Nothing doing, old chap," you say, and lead Watson back to look at the paintings.

▶ *Turn to 20*

BILLIARD BALL '20'

You pick up the blue ball featuring a single stripe and the number 20, and add it to the fourth triangle.

You step back to admire your handiwork and pause.

Watson turns to you, "Where next then, Holmes?"

"I'm not quite sure," you admit. "I had hoped that the missing ball might lead us somewhere... that the number 20 was some sort of clue."

You know only too well that if the pieces of the puzzle don't fit, then you can't be looking at it properly – or rather, you can't be looking at all of it.

A moment to take a step back, perhaps? You look around the room and note two anomalies.

▶ *To investigate the fabric sticking out from underneath the billiard table – Turn to 48*

▶ *To investigate the roll of paper protruding from the back of an armchair – Turn to 63*

FIVE-POINTED LEAVES

You approach the plant with five-pointed leaves. As you round the corner, your eyes catch sight of a handrail and some steps descending in the far corner, partially hidden by plants. Another hidden staircase!

You circle the plant. At first you find nothing, but then your eyes are caught by a glint of white in the soil. It's a coil of paper. You reach down to pick it up. You unravel the paper and see this is another page torn from a book about Ada Lovelace.

You whistle for Watson's attention and then read the text aloud: "The Countess of Lovelace was a close companion of inventor Charles Babbage. The two exchanged numerous letters regarding both his Difference and then his Analytical Engine."

You continue reading. "Importantly, Ada translated a text about the Analytical Engine written by the Italian mathematician L.F. Menabrea. The translation included additional notes, written by the Countess herself, which included an algorithm for the Analytical Engine which would produce the important and influential Bernoulli numbers. An imagining of the algorithm is included below."

Then, written in a different hand, you see:

For the Bernoulli numbers:
1. *Use punched cards to enter your starting values.*
2. *Levers 14, 17B and 19 will allow you to define the divisible sequence.*
3. *Reset the central cog.*
4. *Turn it 10 places anticlockwise.*
5. *Ensure the printer is stocked.*

Keep me

Below this, the paper is torn.

The note is grubby, presumably from being stuck in the soil. All the same, you think you can still spot a muddy thumbprint, accompanied by another small handwritten instruction: 'Keep me'.

You turn to Watson. He has a sentence on the tip of his tongue. Something about the brilliance of it all, you can tell. He swallows it.

► *Turn to 72*

UNDER THE BILLIARD TABLE

You send Watson to investigate the underside of the billiard table. He pulls at the fabric, but to no avail.

"Nothing of interest here, Holmes," he calls back, his voice a little constricted from bending over. "Although, it says it was made in 1885."

Watson climbs out from under the table and stands to face you. "Nothing of note," he says, dusting himself down industriously.

You resist the urge to push at this new '1885' inconsistency and return to surveying the room.

▶ *Investigate the roll of paper protruding from the*
back of an armchair – Turn to 63

FIVE PUNCHED CARDS

You walk up to the stream of punched cards. Watson joins you.

"We need to select five cards to enter," you say, sifting through them.

You consider the punched cards. Each has a different number of holes. You sigh.

Watson looks at you. "I believe we may have–"

You cut him off. "I know."

Together you return to the letter and look at the Engine once more.

▶ *Turn to 109*

ATTIC BEDROOM

At the top of the stairs is a door. It creaks open to reveal a small attic room.

"Rather pokey, wouldn't you say?" Watson says.

"Servants' quarters, I imagine," you respond.

In the centre of the room, the bed lies unmade. Among the sheets you see a gold chain with a small gold-coloured cross. On the bedside table is a bottle of wine and a hunk of bread. The drawer to the bedside table lies open.

With a single stride across the tiny room, you are there. Inside the drawer is a letter, a Holy Bible and a handkerchief.

▶ *Pick up the handkerchief – Turn to 76*

▶ *Examine the letter – Turn to 52*

▶ *Open the Holy Bible – Turn to 101*

SMOKING ROOM

You head to the bottom right-hand window. Watson follows. You climb in and find yourself in a Smoking Room. You scan your surroundings. There are chairs, tables, a cigar cabinet and other cupboards, and a large desk. An ornately carved box sits on a small, low table. You ponder your first move.

▶ *Examine the cigar cabinet – Turn to 5*

▶ *Inspect the desk – Turn to 88*

▶ *Investigate the engraved box – Turn to 3*

㊾ ATTIC LETTER

You pick up the letter.

"1860, Holmes… There is something extraordinary going on, you know. Why is this letter so old?"

"It could easily have been planted for us to find, Watson."

You notice the smudges on the letter. A mother's tears, you think… A cruel master and a hardy Cornishman… You replace the letter.

▶ *Turn to 50*

Langreek Cottage
Talland Hill
Polperro
Cornwall
25th day of June 1860

My dear Tristan,

Thank you, darling, for the cake recipe, and please thank Mrs Clem and everyone in the kitchens. It comforts my heart to think that you are well fed, at least.

I think of you often, labouring for that cruel man. How are you surviving? Dear Tristan, please look for another position. Or come back to us here… all your old friends in Polperro are asking for you and you could work with Uncle Arthur and cousins Dewi and Jacka on the boats.

Your devoted Mam

A STAIRCASE

Opening the blue door reveals a staircase. "Tally ho!" Watson says.

You sigh. The good doctor seems rather excitable today. You follow him long-sufferingly down the stairs.

"By Jove! Extraordinary!" you hear him exclaim.

On arrival at the foot of the stairs, you find a very dusty area with a suit of armour, together with assorted fruits... rhubarb, pears and apples. This is interesting, you admit.

But look – in the dust, the words 'Dead End' are scrawled.

The blue door must have been the wrong choice. What has happened to your mental processes today? You are feeling rather tired. It was not a good night's rest last night, what with the excitement of catching Moran and then all the drilling and banging near 221B Baker Street.

▶ *Turn to 26*

GARDEN SYMMETRY – THREE MISSING

"Well, I think three are missing," you declare, confidently.

"Well done, old man. Quick as a flash!"

But something makes you pause. Are you sure you've got them all?

▶ *You look again – Turn to 66*

THE FIFTH BOOK ON THE FIFTH SHELF IN THE FIFTH BOOKCASE

As Watson hands you the book, it falls open to a central page.

"See here, old chap," you say. You read the page aloud. "For a number of years Charles Babbage collaborated closely with Ada Augusta King, Countess of Lovelace. The Countess's fascination with machinery can be traced back to her childhood, during which she wrote a set of instructions for the creation and operation of a mechanical bird. Please find an imagining of her bird algorithm here."

"Ada Lovelace," he wonders aloud. "Where have I heard that name?"

You give him a few moments to get there. "The coachman!" You nod. There it is. You return to the page and consider the algorithm.

To fly:

1. Take the wheel, start at 'B'.
2. Around the wheel, attach six thin poles in two sets of three.
3. Wind netting around the poles, tightly when close to the wheel, and looser as you move further away. This will form the base of your wings.

Keep me

"Remarkable," Watson swoons. "She designed this when only a child!"

Your mind is elsewhere.

"An algorithm for a mechanical bird, Watson? What relevance does this have to the house? Or our being here? Perhaps we fly out? Is that our escape?" you huff, snapping the book shut. "And see here, this page is inserted. The book is in fact about flora and fauna. There is something at play."

Watson nods but looks confused.

"And," you say, pointing, "a single muddy fingerprint in the corner."

"Like on the envelope?" Watson offers. "How odd."

You peer closely at the fingerprint and note a message written in a very small font. 'Keep me,' it reads.

In one movement you lift the page containing the algorithm from the book and plunge it into your pocket. "Where next?" you ask.

▶ *Turn to 102*

(56) TO THE BALLROOM?

"It could only be 56, Watson. Come along."

Watson does not follow you. "Look here, Holmes, the letters BR are scratched beneath Cube 56."

You can almost hear the gears grinding in his brain.

"So, we go to the Ballroom," you say.

You both clamber out of the trapdoor back into the Hall. Behind you there is a thud. You turn. Across the Hall an envelope has just landed on the doormat. You hear crunching as footsteps recede from the door. You pick up the letter.

"Perhaps that's why we were sent down through a trapdoor?" Watson muses. "To divert us away from any incoming post?"

You are hardly listening. The letter weighs heavy in your hands.

Watson joins you. Your process is almost like clockwork. Watson lifts matches from his pocket and strikes a flame. You wait as the wax seal melts and then gently slide out the letter inside. You read together.

You lower the letter. You are both silent.

"So, it's Alfreds' machine then, not Babbage's?" Watson asks. "And this is definitely Alfreds' house, too? And the letter this morning, that was in his hand?"

You nod three times and then clear your throat.

"How lucky this letter landed at this opportune moment," Watson muses. "And one that lays everything out so clearly!"

"Time really is of the essence," you say. "We'd better get on."

"To where though, Holmes?" Watson asks. "Perhaps we take this into our own hands? Deviate from our given path?"

Watson consults the floor plan. "Look, Alfreds has a room upstairs, perhaps we should explore there?"

▶ *Go upstairs and investigate Alfreds` Bedroom – Turn to 64*

▶ *Go to the Ballroom as instructed – Turn to 100*

Mr Bertram Alfreds,

I cannot begin to tell you how utterly appalled and devastated I am by your empty promises and villainous behaviour.

You told us it would be a simple transaction. A single fee, for the return of our beloved, recently deceased Robert. We have given you all we own, and promised far more than that, but we have been left with nothing.

You gave us hope in our lowest moment, but now we have lost Robert, and any hope of rebuilding our lives. We have lost everything.

You are a cruel and manipulative man. If your 'machine' cannot bring people through the veil, what can it do? What have you created it for? Who else will suffer at your hand?

'X' WILL MARK THE SPOT

"Babbage, Babbage...? The name is familiar..."

"Come along, dear boy, keep up," says Mrs Holmes. "Charles Babbage, the mathematician and mechanical engineer. Designer of both the Difference and the Analytical Engines."

Watson chuckles. "Babbage was also known as 'the reformer of the British postal service'..."

"Yet his letter has taken 24 years to be delivered. Very funny." You allow a smile to touch your lips. "The postmark is clearly a fake," you announce.

But Watson argues that sometimes post can be delivered years late. "It could be genuine," he says. "Why not?"

You read the letter. Your mind is already whirring.

Watson opens a trunk of old belongings. "This stuff is still here. I didn't take it when I moved to Kensington. It's been in these rooms since *The Adventure of the Three Thumbless Thespians*."

"Why did you never write that one up?" you ask.

He smiles sadly. "Well, Mary was ill and then..." He offers you some clothes.

"I'd rather be seen..." you begin, but resign yourself to the usefulness. You quickly don a pair of old trousers and a jacket, and take the coat and hat proffered by the good doctor.

You all sit down to Mrs Hudson's breakfast, then, after saying a swift farewell to Mama, you and Watson head out into Baker Street on a damp April day in 1894.

St Thomas's Lodge,
Regent's Park
London
14 July 1870

To my esteemed countryman, Sherlock Holmes Esquire,

I made great progress with my Analytical Engine and you will surely know that part of it was exhibited twenty seven years ago, in 1843, at the King George III Museum. But my work was never finished. Until now.

I invite you to visit me at St Thomas's Lodge, Regent's Park, where I have left something for you to uncover.

Follow this riddle to access fascinating mathematical – and spiritual – secrets.

By the water, 'X' will mark the spot.
Look for the goddess's point, and head in the opposite direction.
Watch for the 'O', the window is below.
Count the lilies in the pond.
Use the number to count your way down.

Yours respectfully,

Charles Babbage

► *Turn to 21*

(58) LIBRARY BOOKSHELF

from 2

"I can't quite piece it together, Holmes. I know how we got to 'bookshelf', but then, what is this 'u' for?" He's holding *Beowulf* in his hands.

You sigh. Together you return to the missing letters.

► *Turn to 2*

11 STEPS NORTH-WEST AND FIVE HOLES

You collect a punched card with five holes and take 11 steps north-west.

You are now standing at the very edge of the Engine. To your left is a small, narrow corridor that appears to lead directly into the rumbling belly.

Together you move down the corridor towards a small metal contraption.

"This must be it." You push in the punched card.

You wait for the Engine to stop. Then, suddenly and inexplicably, the floor disappears from beneath you. You land with a sudden crash.

You are in a small room with three figures. On your left: Edward White Benson, the Archbishop of Canterbury. On your right: Sudhakara Dvivedi, the Indian mathematician you judged the most brilliant man you had ever met. And ahead: your brother, Mycroft.

Sudhakara reaches out a hand and helps you up. "I am so pleased to see that you survived the Reichenbach event they said had killed you," he says. "What is it now, three years past?"

You smile and nod.

"Alfreds tricked you then, too?" Mycroft asks.

You sigh. The instructions you followed weren't designed to stop the Engine at all, they must have been a trick to get you inside...

Mycroft takes a step back and considers your outfit: "Good Lord! What on earth are you wearing?"

You had entirely forgotten about Watson's oversized trousers and misshapen coat.

"I wouldn't say I was tricked!" you respond indignantly. Although, standing here, locked in the Engine in a misshapen suit from *The Adventure of the Three Thumbless Thespians*, you do rather feel the fool.

Mycroft struggles to contain his grin. "And yet you're here, Sherlock, in this room, with us. I think he got you."

▶ *Turn to 19*

⑥⓪ AT THE TABLE

from 18

You move to sit on a chair. Watson joins you, sitting at the opposite side of the round table.

There is amicable silence for a few moments, shattered by Watson.

"Holmes, if you don't mind me asking, why are we sitting here?"

"Just surveying the room, Watson, working out our next move."

"But the note, Holmes?"

He just won't stop!

"I do believe the note contained instructions for us to follow," he insists.

As much as you hate to admit it, Watson does seem to be speaking sense. You look around one final time and head back to the note.

▶ *Turn to 81*

STAY AND INVESTIGATE

You pull a sheet off a square shape to reveal a desk. The desk is topped with leather bearing a now familiar-looking symbol – a silver sun.

"That's the symbol of the Order," Watson says excitedly. "I have a feeling we're lifting a lid on the plot here, Holmes!"

You're not so sure. You note how temporary it all feels – the furniture is easily found, simply by pulling a sheet away. It has the feel of a trail laid to be discovered.

You look more closely at the desk. A long arrow runs around the outside in a clockwise direction. It begins at a small symbol, which looks similar to those found on the Code Wheel, and ends in a drawing of a clock face set at three o'clock. There is a scrap of paper scrawled with a name. It reads: Edward White Benson.

"This looks like our next task," you say. "I believe these are coded instructions on how to open the safe."

"Or perhaps this is simply a reminder left by our host to himself?" Watson offers. "And we're breaking in?"

Watson glances over the desk again and taps on the text. Your memory is as reliable as ever. "Archbishop of Canterbury, old man. But I wonder why his name is cropping up again?"

You put that aside for a moment and concentrate on the puzzle. A clockwise arrow. A symbol at the start and a clock at the end, showing three o'clock.

Watson is at your shoulder. "I think we start at the symbol."

You lift the Code Wheel from his hands and set about solving the puzzle.

▶ *Turn to the number you discover*

(62) BLUE DOOR

from 31

"It's clearly the blue door," you say.

"Why d'you think that, Holmes?" says Watson, grinning in a rather superior fashion.

Now you think about it, you're not sure what to say. You decide to choose again.

▶ *Turn to 31*

(63) A FLOOR PLAN

You deftly untangle the protruding paper from a fabric pouch on the armchair's back.

Together, you flatten the scroll on the billiard table and consider it closely. It is a floor plan of the property, with each room assigned to a number.

"The room we're in now, the Billiard Room," Watson says, "that has been assigned number 41."

"Indeed," you answer. "The '20' on the billiard ball is telling us where to go next."

"The Trophy Room!" Watson says. "Up the stairs and on the first floor, according to the floor plan."

Rather curious numbering on the floor plan, you think. The numbers are not continuous. Is there any logic behind them?

Watson rolls up the floor plan and tucks it under his right arm. You note a string of coded symbols at the very top – a title, perhaps? But there is no time to investigate. Watson is already scuttling off down the corridor.

▶ *You follow him – Turn to 20*

▶ *(To view the full floor plan – Turn to the back of the book)*

ALFREDS' BEDROOM

You lead the way upstairs at a swift pace to the house's principal bedroom.

"Hurry along, Watson." After your adventures in Tibet, Persia and France you are in superb physical condition and easily outdo the panting doctor, who seems to have been seeking solace in the dining room following your disappearance – and his wife's passing.

Coming through the door behind you, he says, "The room seems sparse – and eerily empty…"

"Of course, the cunning fox hasn't left things out for us to find," you say. "We'll need to track down his hiding place."

"Look!"

There is a message in what looks like a foreign language painted onto the peeling white walls. Curious that the room is not better maintained, you think. The letters all seem muddled. What can it mean?

You look around, alert as ever to a clue or a lead. Across the room, the early morning light is bouncing off a mirror.

Is there another way to read the message?

▶ *Turn to the number you discover*

Take the wheel.
Start at the letter U.
Turn even places
anticlockwise.
Use the number given.

FREEDOM!

You turn the blue handle. There is a grinding noise and a door opens. You lead the way back from the inner chamber into the Engine Room. You are able to close the opening from which you emerge so that it is not obvious that you have all escaped.

Looking around, you think that Alfreds managed to assemble quite an impressive group – three major figures in their fields, plus the ever-resourceful Doctor Watson. And even Mycroft is a public figure of some renown…

Sudhakara Dvivedi is speaking. "My proposal would be for us to conceal ourselves and allow the event organized by Alfreds to go ahead."

"Yes," you say. "He will expect to reveal us – most notably to reveal me, back from the dead – but…"

Watson says "We need to hurry. The event was scheduled for nine o'clock in the morning and it sounds as if they are coming now."

You all scurry around the far side of the machine, where there is a gap large enough to squeeze into, between the Engine and the wall.

You catch a glimpse of the Prime Minister and various dignitaries being ushered into the room by Alfreds (whom you recognize from the portraits earlier), even as you disappear into the shadows.

▶ *Turn to 40*

⟨66⟩ LIBRARY WINDOW

"It appears to tell us to look outside," Watson says.

You move across to the window, which overlooks a garden. As you arrive you see a figure moving just out of sight. The gardener again. It looks as if he is in a rush and carrying something rather heavy. You recognize something about that walk... The light is fading. Time is ticking on.

"I say!" Watson is at your shoulder. "Look at this!" From a chair behind you he picks up a newspaper clipping folded into a paper aeroplane.

Unfolding it, he reads, "Symmetrical Delights at St Thomas's Lodge. The newly appointed gardener at St Thomas's Lodge appears to have brought a mathematician's eye to bear on the landscaped grounds of the house. The gardener, answering only to 'Mr G.', has built a reputation for attractive symmetrical arrangements of plants and flower beds."

There is a muddy fingerprint on the bottom right-hand corner and a handwritten scrawl that asks, 'How many are missing?' You look out of the window once again. Is it 'attractive'? you wonder. Something seems wrong.

"I wonder..." Watson pauses.

"...if we need to work out how many are missing from this arrangement?" you say, stating succinctly what the doctor is struggling to formulate.

"Exactly as I was going to say," Watson claims.

A likely story, you think.

▶ *There are three missing – Turn to 54*

▶ *There are four missing – Turn to 38*

▶ *There are five missing – Turn to 99*

BUTTON 67

"I think it must be 67!" you exclaim. You reach for the box, but Watson stops you.

"I'm not sure that's right, Holmes, because that would make…" Watson trails off as he sees your expression.

You feel slow, slightly confused. Perhaps your hurried return to solve what Watson is already calling *The Adventure of the Empty House* is taking its toll. Only a few days ago you were in Montpellier in the south of France. You look again at the statements. Watson is indeed correct.

► *Turn to 3*

"THE LANGUAGE OF THE SILVER SUN"

Watson turns the dial with precision. The arrow slows and then lands on '68'. The box clicks open.

You peer inside and pull out a small, grubby piece of paper. There are four words followed by a single line of symbols.

"For those who dare…" Watson reads aloud. You say nothing – it's the symbols that interest you.

"Get out the Code Wheel, Watson. No time to waste. We've got a message to decode."

Watson takes the Wheel out of his pocket and sets about entering symbols and noting down letters. He's holding the Wheel so it is facing you. You observe the back.

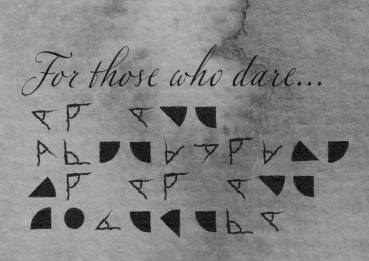

For those who dare...

You see a single sentence written twice – first in symbols, then in letters.

"The Order's code," you read. "The Language of the Silver Sun."

That must be it. The symbols are a coded language. Messages left to members of the Order of the Silver Sun.

Watson lowers the Wheel. He is done. You consider the message and look around the room to work out your next move.

▶ *Head to the window – Turn to 92*

▶ *Head to the Scullery – Turn to 32*

▶ *Head to the staircase – Turn to 78*

69 BIBLE MESSAGE – "WILL"

You put down your pencil and read the message one last time. Although you're not sure you can call it a message, really – it's just a jumble of words.

Frustrated, you begin to pace up and down the wooden floorboards.

"What are we missing?" you say, turning sharply on your heel. "The sequence of numbers written at the top of the page is trying to show us a hidden message in the text. Correct?" Watson nods.

"The numbers must be showing us where the words we need to find are positioned. Correct?" Watson nods again.

"So, what do the three numbers mean?" you ask. "Line numbers? Paragraphs? Word in a sentence? Number of times the word appears on the page...?" You trail off.

Watson is nodding, but you don't notice – you're back, pencil in hand, trying to decode the message.

▶ *Turn to 101*

70 CARRIAGE 741

You spot Carriage 741 in the distance and raise your hand to get the coachman's attention. He pulls the carriage to a standstill and you gather your coat, ready to climb in. Watson doesn't follow you. You look back at him quizzically. He is staring at the number on the side.

"I don't think the odd numbers are together there, Holmes," he says.

You look again and, by Jove, he is right. You sheepishly wave the driver on and return to the envelope.

► *Turn to 21*

⑦¹ GO RIGHT

"I believe we need to go right," Watson says, pointing to the grey door next to you.

He moves towards the door and you follow, allowing your hands to brush against the bannister as you do.

You stop. "Watson," you say. "Just here I can feel a single dot. An 'E' in Morse code. I don't think 'right' can be correct."

Watson consults the alphabet in his hands and then nods. He rejoins you on the stairs and together you take another look at the puzzle.

► *Turn to 93*

A SMALL BLACK BOX

You sigh deeply as you roll up the paper and drop it into your pocket.

Watson turns to face you. "We need to find and stop Alfreds' engine. Yes?"
You nod. "We know it's going to cause harm. Someone is coming back from
the dead, through the veil. And it is somehow connected to his –"

"Ridiculous," you interject.

"... Order." Watson finishes. "The Order of the Silver Sun."

"But, why am I being given these algorithms?" you muse.

Watson shrugs. You stand together for a moment.

"You know, Holmes," Watson turns to you, a glint in his eye. "The
Bernoulli numbers are really something marvellous. Pervasive and present,
they appear in a great variety of mathematical fields. That must be why the
Countess chose them for the algorithm she wrote for Babbage's machine."

You let him run out of steam and then nod. "Yes, I know."

Over his shoulder, something catches your eye. A small black box. You walk
towards it, lift it up, shake it, try to prise it open. There is a circular dial on
the front. A ring surrounded by numbers. It's locked. As you turn it over,
you note some text – a message. It reads: 'Cast your mind back to 221B.
Remember the letter. Be bold, Holmes.'

You motion to Watson. "Alfreds' letter from breakfast. Get it out. We're
going to need it."

▶ *To consult Alfreds' letter, turn to 57, then turn*
to the number you discover

TILE 73

from 29

You reach for Tile 73, but to your surprise you feel Watson's hand holding you back.

You turn to face him. "Yes?" you ask. "What?"

"That's not the right tile, Holmes," Watson responds. You are a little taken aback by his directness. "I am positive the single tile at the top is part of the sequence."

You realize he is correct.

"I know, Watson," you retort, a trifle infuriated. "Let's just focus on solving this puzzle and finding our way out of here."

▶ *Turn to 29*

BOTTOM LEFT-HAND WINDOW

from 98

You work your way through Babbage's instructions, turn on your heel and head towards the bottom left-hand window.

Watson is at your left elbow.

"The finger, Holmes," he says, pointing. "We should be going in the other direction."

You sigh, deeply, return to the 'X' and look at Babbage's instructions again.

▶ *Turn to 98*

AN UNVEILING

Watson is holding one of the papers he has picked up from the Drawing Room rug.

"I say," he murmurs, "it's about this very house. It appears to be an invitation..." He holds it up for you to read.

"Leading members of the Establishment, including the Prime Minister, the Foreign Secretary, members of the Diogenes Club, and the mysteriously missing Archbishop of Canterbury, have reported to *The Gazette* that they have received the following invitation..."

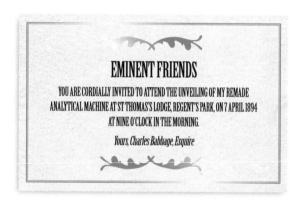

EMINENT FRIENDS

YOU ARE CORDIALLY INVITED TO ATTEND THE UNVEILING OF MY REMADE
ANALYTICAL MACHINE AT ST THOMAS'S LODGE, REGENT'S PARK, ON 7 APRIL 1894
AT NINE O'CLOCK IN THE MORNING.

Yours, Charles Babbage, Esquire

"...The invitees note that Mr Babbage – celebrated inventor of the Difference Engine – died on 18 October 1871. The notes were all postmarked 7 April 1870."

You look at the clock. It is a few minutes to four o'clock. Where has the time gone? Perhaps those forty winks you snatched took a little longer than you thought... which means you have only five hours left. You thrive on being challenged and Watson, too, is a very good man under pressure. But still: chop, chop, you think.

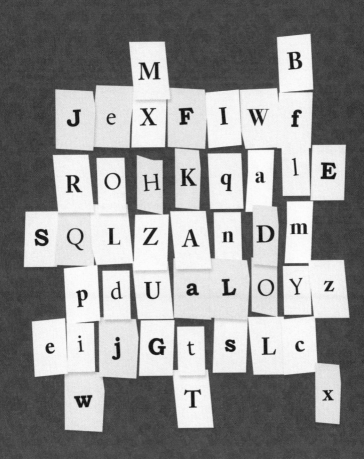

Watson is calling you over to the far wall. "Looks like a random collection of letters," he says. "But look, old chap – underneath someone's written, 'Where next, Holmes?'"

Perhaps you can find the name of a room among the jumbled letters and use the floor plan to find your next location?

▶ *Turn to the number you discover*

(76) ATTIC HANDKERCHIEF

You pick up the handkerchief. A small piece of machinery rolls out onto your palm. You notice at once that it is slightly chipped and there is some quite fresh oil on it.

You show Watson.

Is this the fourth machine part you have been presented with?

▶ *Turn to 50*

TROPHY CABINET

The clues appear to lead to the trophy cabinet. You inspect its contents closely. There are various engraved cups congratulating Charles Babbage on his success in school competitions – a mathematics prize, a Latin prize, one for natural sciences. Hidden behind the cups are a collection of small portraits, always of the same two friends.

"I say," Watson says, "Isn't this a young...?"

As usual, you are there before him. "Moriarty, yes." You shudder.

But who is the other fellow with him? Neither you nor Watson have any idea.

Watson interrupts your reverie. "Do you know, Holmes, I know a very great deal about the wonderful Charles Babbage and I do believe he was home tutored, so how could he win school prizes?"

You are silent.

"Look at this," he says. He has a card in his hand that reads: 'Try Again.'

▶ *You return to examine the portraits – Turn to 20*

A BASEMENT SURPRISE

You lead Watson around the plants to the hidden staircase. Together you begin to descend. Beneath your feet the stairs are trembling gently.

"Where is he leading us, Holmes?"

You say nothing. The odd algorithms weigh heavily in your pocket. You can't quite work them out... who they are from, what they are for? You know all too well that this dissonance is telling you something. What are you missing? What have you not understood?

You reach the bottom of the stairs. The tremble is now a loud rumble.

In front of you is a long corridor with heavy oak doors at the end. You can see the doors shaking on their hinges. The room beyond must hold whatever is causing the rumbling. This is where you are headed.

You begin to walk towards the door. Watson follows.

As you walk you note piles of cogs and dirty rags littered across the floor, and then, on your right, a large toolbox. You pause. Something catches in your memory. A toolbox?

You're reminded of a 'Watch out!' and for a second you're sure you feel plush satin beneath your fingertips. Your nose is engulfed by a floral scent. What memory did the toolbox unlock?

The rumbling reverberates in your ears. Not much time left before the event. You wonder what to do next.

▶ *Investigate the toolbox – Turn to 105*

▶ *Keep moving towards the door – Turn to 109*

IN THE STUDY

Watson follows you to the Study. It is a large room, sparsely furnished. There is a round wooden table against one wall and various other protruding shapes, which appear to be pieces of furniture covered in white sheets.

On the table you note a number of sheets of paper. One has the words 'The Order of the Silver Sun – travel back through the veil' on it. You note a silver circle above a flat line – a rising sun? The symbol of the Order?

You remember Alfreds' letter. It said: 'The veil between the land of the living and the land of the dead is not as solid as we once thought.' A journey back through the veil... what might that mean? No time for that now.

You return to the table. To the right, there is a second sheet, which features a number of diagrams and a question mark.

"We need to find the missing number," Watson offers, pointing to the question mark.

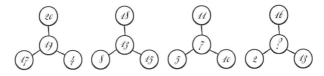

"I do believe each of these triangular shapes follow the same pattern," you muse aloud. "There is some rule to combine the three outside numbers to create the number within."

"So, we need to find the rule and then apply it here?" Watson asks, tapping the question mark.

You set about solving the puzzle.

▶ *Turn to the number you discover*

"So, I'll be his proof?" you ask.

"Indeed," the Archbishop responds.

"The great Sherlock Holmes returned from the dead," Mycroft scoffs.

"We need to find a way out of here," you say. "His plan can't succeed."

"Where are we, in fact?" Watson asks.

"Work it out, man! We're inside the confounded machine," Mycroft replies testily.

"I've been working on the Engine from the inside," Dvivedi offers, "but I haven't been able to find any way out. I'm primarily just resolving his mathematical errors."

You look around the room and note something engraved into the wall. A message, below which are three handles, each a different colour.

"Have you tried these?" you ask, reaching for one.

"Don't!" they all exclaim, simultaneously.

"I'm familiar with this type of locking system," Dvivedi tells you. "The correct handle will allow us to escape, but a wrong one will send the whole machine into lock-down. We have a single chance."

You nod, and step closer to consider the message.

Below the text you see three handles: one blue, one green and one yellow.

You consider the text. Ada... her name echoes back across the night, connecting clue, fact, algorithm and muddy fingerprint...

For *A* *D* *A*

What colour, enchantress of numbers?

"I'm surprised that your green-fingered lady friend didn't help you," Mycroft chuckles.

"You mean Irene Adler, masquerading as the gardener and our coachman?"

Mycroft is silent. Watson looks stunned.

"On the contrary, Irene's muddy fingerprints have been a huge help. Those and the Countess of Lovelace. If I'm not mistaken, Ada is our key."

You take a deep breath and reach for one of the handles.

► *You turn the blue handle – Turn to 65*

► *You turn the green handle – Turn to 95*

► *You turn the yellow handle – Turn to 25*

CONSERVATORY

"My, oh my," Watson breathes. "This is a surprise."

You come into a conservatory. It's filled with a soothing dawn light, although you are less soothed by the thought of a rapidly approaching morning.

Has a mathematical eye been at work again? Interesting how the leaves of each plant have a different number of points. It's all quite pleasing, really.

"What's that line, Watson? About a green thought in a green shade?"

"Andrew Marvell, Holmes, the metaphysical poet..."

"Ah yes, Milton's friend."

"'Annihilating all that's made To a green thought in a green shade.' Quite beautiful."

You see the note on the table long before Watson points it out.

Let's not stay PENT up
Eh, Sherlock?
A moment to engage with
the senses?
*Find all the **vowels**,*
they'll show you the way.

He takes it and shows it to you, pointing to a smudge. "Dirt, Watson," you opine. "A gardener's hands... again..."

Watson looks at you quizzically, but you think you might just have it.

► *Move towards the plant with five-pointed leaves – Turn to 47*

► *Move towards the plant with three-pointed leaves – Turn to 104*

► *Sit on a chair – Turn to 60*

BUTTON 82

"If not 28, then perhaps 82?" Watson offers.

You look at the statements, nodding. On first glance, you can see no issue.

You run through the statements one by one for a final check. The third snags. It doesn't work after all. You begin again.

► *Turn to 3*

BILLIARD BALL 'K'

Your hand hovers over the ball and you run one final check in your head. Colour, yes, stripe, yes, but... the 'K'? And the square, too?

Doubt pulls your hand back to your side, and you return to the sequence to consider it once more.

► *Turn to 41*

BIBLE MESSAGE – 'THY'

"Thy," you say, marking the final word and laying down your pencil. You move briskly away from the Bible and begin to look around the room.

"What can it mean?" you muse aloud. Watson doesn't respond, he's still staring at the Bible, tapping numbers and words with his fingers.

Then he stands up and turns to you.

"I don't think that 'thy' can be right, Holmes," he says. "The message doesn't make sense. I don't think we've understood the number sequence correctly."

You walk over to join him. A little dejected, you run through the numbers in your head: Chapter 26, 11 disciples, paragraph eight, line, word, 'He'.

You pick up your pencil and begin the task once more.

► *Turn to 101*

CARRIAGE 147

You spot Carriage 147 turning onto Baker Street. You're in luck! You raise your hand to signal to the coachman, then you stop and look again at the numbers printed on the carriage's side.

The gap between the first two numbers is three for sure, but it looks as though the two odd numbers are in fact separated here. Watson doesn't seem to have noticed your slip up, however, so you cough, by way of a distraction, and return to the envelope.

▶ *Turn to 21*

PINK DOOR

You're at something of a loss and pick the pink door. Watson tags along obediently down the corridor. He tries it, but it is locked and will not budge, no matter how hard he shoves.

You're able to save face by reprimanding him for his military ways.

"Brute force will not help, Watson," you say, tapping the side of your head.

He scowls as you return to consider the puzzle.

▶ *Turn to 31*

BACK AT BAKER STREET

"The Bernoulli numbers!" you exclaim, reading the report in *The Evening Gazette*. "Most remarkable!"

"Yes," says Sudhakara Dvivedi. "In spite of himself, Alfreds achieved something with that machine."

"Very generous of you to say that," says Watson, "but it was surely the design excellence of Mr Babbage, and the ideas of Ada Lovelace that bore fruit."

"And also, of course, the amendments you made to the running of the machine while locked up inside it," you say.

"That is all true," says Dvivedi. "And I must say, it is good to see the Engine returned to its mathematical purpose. It was utterly wasted as a prop in Alfreds' fanciful plot."

"Some more tea, Mr Dvivedi?" says Mrs Hudson.

"Thank you, yes," he says.

You all gather around to reread the report of the unveiling in *The Evening Gazette*.

"Baker Street maestro... Very nice," you chuckle.

THE END

The Evening Gazette

7 April 1894

HOLMES ALIVE! DETECTIVE EMERGES FROM HIDING TO FOIL DESPICABLE 'ANALYTICAL ENGINE' SWINDLE, SAVES GOVERNMENT THOUSANDS

ENGINE'S CLAIMED POWER TO DEFEAT DEATH SHOWN TO BE FAKE

CHARLATAN BERTRAM ALFREDS UNDER ARREST

In extraordinary scenes in St Thomas's Lodge, Regent's Park, this morning the Baker Street maestro Sherlock Holmes unmasked 'Metaphysical Engineer' Mr Bertram Alfreds as a charlatan, thereby saving the government a large sum of money.

Prime Minister Lord Rosebery welcomed the news that Holmes had remarkably survived his encounter at the Reichenbach Falls three years ago and thanked him personally, praising his great powers of... (Continued on page 3.)

MACHINE PRINTS BERNOULLI NUMBERS

In the aftermath of the unmasking and arrest of Mr Bertram Alfreds (described left), notable Indian mathematician Mr Sudhakara Dvivedi demonstrated that the Analytical Engine on the premises – built by Alfreds from the plans of Mr Charles Babbage – was printing the mathematically important Bernoulli numbers. Dvivedi said, "I was able to make various improvements to the machine on the basis of notes left by Countess Ada Lovelace and found they worked, and the machine delivered the Bernoulli numbers, which is a major development for mathematicians because... (Continued on page 5.)

GARDENER MISSING

Those involved in the dramatic events at St Thomas's Lodge (described left) applauded the help provided by a recently appointed gardener. However, a *Gazette* reporter discovered that said gardener disappeared early this morning, leaving no trace.

PROGRESS IN PARK LANE MURDER

Inspector Lestrade of Scotland Yard announced the arrest of Colonel Sebastian Moran as the murderer of the Honourable Ronald Adair on March 30 in the famous Park Lane Mystery. The Inspector paid tribute to an anonymous helper and also thanked Dr John Watson, former associate of Sherlock Holmes.

(88) DESK

On the desk you find a pile of papers, several inkpots and a heavy fountain pen. You sift through the papers. One contains a long list of dates, times and locations. There are three sets of initials written in the lower left-hand corner: M.H., S.D. and E.W.B.

Beneath this, there is another sheet with a single line of text that reads, 'The Order of the Silver Sun'.

You call Watson over. "Have you heard this phrase before? The Order of the Silver Sun?" Watson shakes his head.

Your eyes rest on the papers. They appear to be written in the same hand as Babbage's letter. Curious. You roll the papers up, slip them in your pocket and return to surveying the room.

▶ *Examine the cigar cabinet – Turn to 5*

▶ *Investigate the engraved box – Turn to 3*

(89) 'D'

"It's quite straightforward, Watson – it's 'D'," you say.

"I'm not sure I agree with you, Holmes," Watson says, slowly shaking his head from side to side in a patronizing way. "If you look…"

Intolerable. You both go back to the puzzle.

▶ *Turn to 43*

(90) STEPLADDER

You work through Babbage's instructions methodically, and confidently head towards the stepladder. As you do, your eye is caught by a pink water lily floating on the pond's surface. You hadn't noticed it before.

You stop, return to the 'X' and look at the letter again.

▶ *Turn to 98*

IN THE SCULLERY

You lead the way into the Scullery, Watson following closely behind. You see something – a parchment roll? – on a high shelf above the sink, just out of reach. Stretching to get it, you knock a vase off the shelf and even with your cat-like reflexes you're unable to avoid it hitting your head...

And the rest is... darkness.

"Holmes! Holmes!"

You wake to see Inspector Lestrade's incredulous face.

"He's coming round at last – at last. Thank God." Watson sounds rather worried.

Your head is aching. "How long was I out?"

"Getting on for five hours," Lestrade says.

"I'm so sorry, Holmes," Watson pants. "You knocked that heavy pot off the shelf and were out cold..."

"What were you two doing in Mr Alfreds' villa anyway? And hiding away in the Scullery?" Lestrade goes on. "If you were in the villa, why weren't you attending the presentation?"

Your brain is recovering: "Of the Analytical Engine? What happened?"

"It turns out the Analytical Engine is a fraud, Holmes. And Bertram Alfreds, a charlatan. Your mother foiled the plot. With the help of a handsome young coachman, who we haven't been able to identify. The Archbishop of Canterbury, your brother Mycroft and an Indian mathematician named Sudhakara Dvivedi were discovered inside the machine, having been fooled and humiliated by Alfreds.

"Dvivedi!" Watson says. "Isn't he the chap you said was the cleverest man you had ever met?"

"Well, he certainly was talking over my head," says Lestrade. "Something about how he got the Engine working and it was printing Bentoully numbers or something…"

"Bernoulli," you say. You groan. Mama. At least Mycroft was fooled, you think. You close your eyes and wish you could disappear into an opium den.

► *Turn to 106*

⓽② TO THE WINDOW

from 32, 68

You walk over to the window.

It's getting to be very light outside. A whole night has passed. What does Alfreds have planned? you wonder.

You watch the garden for a few moments. Looking for a sign, a clue… Perhaps a figure in the dawn light? Watson comes to join you.

"Holmes?"

"There's nothing to see here," you turn to him. "I believe we have come to the wrong spot."

Together, you return to the scrap of paper and consider the symbols once more.

► *Turn to 68*

"'Z' is correct," Watson says, "but I have no idea where to go next."

You ponder. "Does the letter 'Z' suggest anything?" Of course, you think. "Come on, old chap," you say, as you lead him down the staircase. At the bottom of the stairs there is a door ahead and others to the left and right. You stop. You feel rather directionless – and tired.

"Where do you think, Holmes?" Watson asks.

"Perhaps," you start, but no words follow.

You turn away and lean on the banister for support. As you do, your fingertip brushes against a small indentation. You peer closer. There is a single short line carved into the wood. A theory begins to form. You move your hand along the bannister – there are indentations there, too!

"Watson!" you call. "Get out your Morse code notes. We've got a message here."

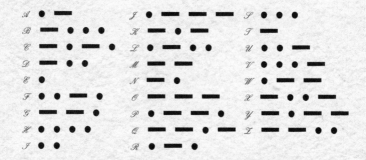

► *Turn left – Turn to 23*

► *Go straight ahead – Turn to 14*

► *Turn right – Turn to 71*

(94) CUBE 94

from 18

"94," you say.

Watson consults the floor plan. "I'm not sure. Shall we look again?"

You both examine the cubes once more.

► *Turn to 18*

(95) GREEN HANDLE

from 80

"Green," you say.

"Are you sure, Mr Holmes?" Sudhakara Dvivedi says. "Let's not be hasty."

You are sure of your choice. You turn the green handle. Nothing happens. Dvivedi looks away. Mycroft groans loudly.

► *Turn to 11*

BUTTON 96

You press Button 96. The box springs open.

Watson reaches into the box and pulls out a large metal disc covered in interlocking cogs of different sizes. You lift out the letter sitting beneath it.

Watson examines the device. "I do believe this is a Code Wheel, Holmes," he says. "Numbers, colours, letters, and then these strange markings... I'm not sure I've seen anything like these before..."

Watson inspects the mechanism closely, turning a couple of the cogs. He quickly grows bored and places it in his pocket.

You open the letter in your hand and read it aloud. Just as you finish reading, there is an almighty bang. Behind you the window slams shut and a key turns in the lock. Wheeling around, you catch sight of a man moving away, a slender arm, a flash of grey hair and the flick of a tailcoat.

Watson rushes to the window and wrestles with it for a few moments before turning to you. "Goodness Holmes, I do believe we're locked in."

"Indeed, old chum," you say. "Someone is pretty keen on getting and keeping us here."

"We should really start looking for a way to escape!"

You don't move. "I do believe the key lies in finding the Engine. This 'B' fellow clearly wants us to look at it."

"Charles Babbage, Holmes."

"I wouldn't be so sure, Watson," you respond. "This letter has today's date."

"Spectres of those who have passed!" Watson exclaims, gesturing to the letter.

St Thomas's Lodge,
Regent's Park,
London
6 April 1894

To my esteemed guests,

What a joy it is to have you here, in the flesh no less. Not
something I thought would be possible, Mr Holmes, unless
you are indeed joining us from beyond the grave.

There will be a few of us here today – spectres of those who
have passed. The veil between the land of the living and the
land of the dead is not as solid as we once thought.

I have something to show you, but you'll need to prove
yourself first. There are challenges for you, and you'll
need to play your cards right, Holmes, or you might find
yourself passing back through the veil.

Let's start with some food and drink. Take the door. I'll see
you in the Dining Room.

Your host,

B

"The date doesn't tell us anything, Holmes. For all we know, Charles
Babbage could be here in this very room!"

What's come over Watson? you think. As a man of science, he has never
been one to believe in spectres from the past.

"To the Dining Room?" you ask. The good doctor follows.

▶ Turn to 26

AT THE HOLMES' RESIDENCE

"Some more tea, Mr Dvivedi?" says Mrs Holmes. "And some of my favourite lemon cake?"

"Thank you, yes," he says, adjusting his position on your mother's couch.

"The Bernoulli numbers!" she exclaims. "Most remarkable!"

"Yes," says Sudhakara Dvivedi. "In spite of himself, Alfreds achieved something with that machine."

"Very generous of you to say that," says your mother, "but it was surely the design excellence of Mr Babbage, and the ideas of Ada Lovelace that bore fruit."

"And also, of course, the amendments you made to the running of the machine while locked up inside it," you say.

"That is all true," says Dvivedi. "And I must say, it is good to see the Engine returned to its mathematical purpose. It was utterly wasted as a prop in Alfreds' fanciful plot."

You all gather around, rather apprehensively, to reread the report of the unveiling in *The Evening Gazette*.

► *THE END*

The Evening Gazette

HOLMES ALIVE – BUT SHAMED

FAMOUS DETECTIVE'S MOTHER FOILS DESPICABLE 'ANALYTICAL ENGINE' SWINDLE, SAVES GOVERNMENT THOUSANDS

HOLMES HIMSELF FOOLED, CAPTURED AND HUMILIATED

CHARLATAN BERTRAM ALFREDS UNDER ARREST

As often before, a member of the Holmes family prevented a major crime this morning. However, it was not the great detective Sherlock or his brother Mycroft, but their mother Mrs Agatha Effie Theodora Holmes of Knightsbridge, who saved the day when she uncovered the much-vaunted 'Metaphysical Engineer' Mr Bertram Alfreds as a charlatan, saving the government a large sum of money.

Meanwhile, the Holmes brothers were discovered locked away having been fooled and humiliated by Alfreds. Prime Minister Lord Rosebery welcomed the extraordinary news that Sherlock had survived his encounter at the Reichenbach Falls but regretted the apparent decline in the detective's powers. He thanked Mrs Holmes personally, praising her great powers of... (Continued on page 3.)

(Continued on page 3.)

MACHINE PRINTS BERNOULLI NUMBERS

In the aftermath of the unmasking and arrest of Mr Bertram Alfreds (described left), notable Indian mathematician Mr Sudhakara Dvivedi demonstrated that the Analytical Engine on the premises – built by Alfreds from the plans of Mr Charles Babbage – was printing the mathematically important Bernoulli numbers. Dvivedi said, "I was able to make various improvements to the machine on the basis of notes left by Countess Ada Lovelace and found they worked and the machine delivered the Bernoulli numbers, which is a major development for mathematicians because... (Continued on page 5.)

(Continued on page 5.)

COACHMAN SOUGHT

Mrs Holmes applauded the help provided by a mysterious and strikingly handsome coachman, who provided key elements of information to enable her to crack the plot. However, *The Gazette* has discovered no trace of any handsome coachman on the streets of London this day in April 1894.

PROGRESS IN PARK LANE MURDER

Inspector Lestrade of Scotland Yard announced the arrest of Colonel Sebastian Moran as the murderer of the Honourable Ronald Adair on March 30 in the famous Park Lane Mystery. The Inspector paid tribute to an anonymous helper and also thanked Dr John Watson, former associate of Sherlock Holmes.

IN THE GARDEN

"This is as far as I can get you," the coachman says. "You'll need to find your own way from here."

He points through the trees and you note an outline of a house beyond the branches. Watson hands the man his fare, and together you head into the gardens, walking towards the property.

After a couple of minutes, the trees thin out. The house is visible in front of you. Watson consults the letter. "This must be it, Holmes," he says, turning to you. "We have followed the instructions exactly."

You look around, searching for the clues – an 'X', the water, a goddess...

The 'water', you imagine, is the small pond, and there are a number of lilies in it. In the centre of the pond, a goddess, but you're yet to find the 'X'...

"Holmes, here!" Watson calls, pointing at a small 'X' in the dirt.

You position yourself on the 'X', facing the house. Your eyes scan the windows and you notice a small stepladder resting against one of the walls. You pray you won't have to use it.

Your mind runs through the instructions one final time: By the water, 'X' will mark the spot. Look for the goddess's point, and head in the opposite direction. Watch for the 'O', the window is below. Count the lilies in the pond. Use the number to count your way down.

You set about locating the correct window.

▶ *Climb into the bottom left-hand window – Turn to 74*

▶ *Climb into the bottom right-hand window – Turn to 51*

▶ *Climb into the window with the chandelier – Turn to 90*

(99) GARDEN SYMMETRY - FIVE MISSING

"Five is the correct answer," you say. "Do you see?" you explain. "One at the top, one at the bottom, one at the left and two on the right."

Watson nods. But what does five mean?

You turn from the window and begin to pace. The puzzle considered how objects are laid out in space... so where is five in this room? You look around again.

The bookshelves all have numbers on. And you could count the number of shelves and the number of books.

You explain to Watson: "Try the fifth bookshelf, the fifth shelf, the fifth book."

"I say, would you count from the bottom or the top? And from the left or the right?"

"Use your eyes, Watson. There are nine shelves of nine books, so count from the top or the bottom and from the left or the right. Please hand me the fifth book on the fifth shelf in the fifth bookcase."

▶ Turn to 55

A VIEW OF THE BALLROOM

You follow Watson downstairs. He fidgets and checks his watch anxiously.

At the bottom of the stairs Watson turns to face you, "Are we any closer to finding this engine, Holmes?" There is a touch of genuine fear in his voice. "We just seem to be climbing up and down staircases!"

You don't say anything in response. What is there to say? You move past him to the Ballroom door and peer through the window. It is grander than you'd expected but a little dilapidated. Chandeliers hang from the ceiling and dawn light streams through the large windows, casting shadows across the parquet flooring. It strikes you that quite a lot of time may now have passed since your forty winks. You aren't entirely sure how long you have left. April dawn in London, you think. Perhaps 5:30am? Which would leave you three and a half hours?

In front of you there is a message pinned to the wooden door. It reads: 'How many different squares can you see, Mr Holmes? Look closely.'

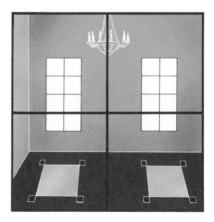

Your eyes scan the room, storing the squares one by one.

▶ *Turn to the number you discover*

ATTIC BIBLE

The Bible is covered in worn black leather and the pages are so thin they are almost translucent.

You flick through it absentmindedly and your eye is caught by a page folded at the corner. At the top you see a list of small numbers written in pencil. They are separated by brackets and commas – perhaps they are instructions of some sort? Beside the first set of numbers is a single word: 'He'.

You look at the page with a sharper eye.

The text is broken into numbered paragraphs, each of which consists of a couple of lines. Perhaps some part of the numbered, bracketed code refers to the paragraphs? Or the lines? Or the words?

You gesture to Watson to join you and together you set about decoding the message.

▶ *If you think the last word is 'will' – Turn to 69*

▶ *If you think the last word is 'more' – Turn to 7*

▶ *If you think the last word is 'thy' – Turn to 84*

The fall of Tyrus is foretold

8 He shall slay with the sword thy daughters in the field : and he shall make a fort against thee, and cast a mount against thee, and lift up the buckler against thee.

9 And he shall set engines of war against thy walls, and with his axes he shall break down thy towers.

10 By reason of the abundance of his horses their dust shall cover thee : thy walls shall shake at the noise of the horsemen, and of the wheels, and of the chariots, when he shall enter into thy gates, as men enter into a city wherein is made a breach.

11 With the hoofs of his horses shall he tread down all thy streets: he shall slay thy people by the sword, and thy strong garrisons shall go down to the ground.

12 And they shall make a spoil of thy riches, and make a prey of thy merchandise: and they shall break down thy walls, and destroy thy pleasant houses: and they shall lay thy stones and thy timber and thy dust in the midst of the water.

13 And I will cause the noise of thy songs to cease; and the sound of thy harps shall be no more heard.

14 And I will make thee like the top of a rock: thou shalt be a *place* to spread nets upon; thou shalt be built no more: for I the LORD have spoken *it*, saith the Lord GOD.

15 Thus saith the Lord GOD to Tyrus; Shall not the isles shake at the sound of thy fall, when the wounded cry, when the slaughter is made in the midst of thee?

16 Then all the princes of the sea shall come down from their thrones, and lay away their robes, and put off their broidered garments: they shall close themselves with trembling: they shall sit upon the ground, and shall tremble at *every* moment, and be astonished at thee.

17 And they shall take up a lamentation for thee, and say to thee, How art thou destroyed, *that wast* inhabited of seafaring men, the renowned city, which wast strong in the sea, she and her inhabitants, which cause their terror to be on all that haunt it!

18 Now shall the isles tremble in the day of thy fall; yea, the isles that are in the sea shall be troubled at thy departure.

19 For thus saith the Lord GOD ; When I shall make thee a desolate city, like the cities that are not inhabited; when I shall bring up the deep upon thee, and great waters shall cover thee;

20 When I shall bring thee down with them that descend into the pit, with the people of old time, and shall set thee in the low parts of the earth, in places desolate of old, with them that go down to the pit, that thou be not inhabited: and I shall set glory in the land of the living ;

21 I will make thee a terror, and thou shalt be no more: though thou be sought for, yet shalt thou never be found again, saith the Lord GOD.

THE ADVENTURE OF THE ANALYTICAL ENGINE

"NO TIME FOR TEA"

"It's rather odd, isn't it?" Watson muses. "All the other puzzles have had such clear instructions. But now I'm totally lost. Almost as though the gardener's missing plants and the hidden algorithm weren't part of the trail..." he stops. Something has caught his eye.

Watson is standing in front of a green book propped up on a display table. "*Great Expectations*," he reads.

Watson opens the book to the first page. It is covered in writing. In the top right-hand corner there is a stamp that reads, 'Property of the Hermetic Order of the Golden Dawn.' The second part of the sentence has been crossed out and replaced with 'Order of the Silver Sun'. Below is a paragraph of text.

"How confusing!" Watson exclaims, but you are already somewhere else entirely.

You decode the passage to find your next location and consult the floor plan to find out where to go next.

► *Turn to the number you discover*

PROPERTY OF
~~THE HERMETIC ORDER~~
~~OF THE GOLDEN DAWN~~
Order of the Silver Sun

For your next location
Root in the word **steady**.
Engage with the initials
No time for tea
Cut it, and instead put YOU.
Holding its place, keep it informal

from 109

⑩ FOUR STEPS NORTH AND TEN HOLES

"I think I know what we need to do," you say.

You walk up to the stream of punched cards and select one with ten holes.

Starting at the circle on the floor, you take four steps in a northerly direction. You look around. You are standing in the centre of the room. There's nowhere to insert the punched card and no obvious way to access the Engine.

You return to Watson. You must have made an error. You consider the Engine again.

▶ *Turn to 109*

⑩ THREE-POINTED LEAVES

from 81

You begin to move towards the plant with three-pointed leaves, the words of the note still running through your mind.

Pent up? Engage with the senses? Whoever wrote this seems far too interested in your emotional state at this moment for your liking! But then...

You stop.

Perhaps you've misunderstood the whole thing. Maybe it's not about being pent up or engaging with your senses at all.

You return to the note for another look.

▶ *Turn to 81*

105 TOOLBOX

You bend down to investigate the toolbox. Watson is at your elbow.

"I thought the coachman's words were a little out of place at the time, but now..."

You sift through the tools and, as expected, uncover another coil of paper.

You unravel it and read aloud: "In the latter part of her life, the Countess of Lovelace was a prolific gambler. She took a particular interest in horse races, building a mathematical system in an attempt to 'beat the odds'. An imagining of the Countess of Lovelace's gambling algorithm is included below."

You note a muddy fingerprint and the words 'Keep me'. Below this the paper is ripped.

You pocket the algorithm and walk towards the rumbling noise.

► *Turn to 109*

1. Take the number given and turn the Wheel clockwise by this number.
2. Enter in odds from past four documented races.
3. Use broker tables to scale for bias.

Keep me

106 IN LESTRADE'S COACH

The coach rattles over the cobbles as Lestrade transports you both to Scotland Yard. Your head is still very sore. Watson is too attentive, and endlessly apologetic, but Lestrade is treating you with an amused condescension. It's really too much after you helped him solve the Park Lane murder only two days ago.

You stop on a corner and he jumps out to get the first edition of *The Evening Gazette*. He is rather too keen to show you the less than flattering account of events and will not meet your eye when you ask how the journalist discovered what happened to you and Watson in such detail.

You read the final item. Handsome coachman? That chap who is driving us now was rather handsome, and, you reflect, he had a familiar look to him...

▶ *THE END*

The Evening Gazette

HOLMES ALIVE – BUT NO LONGER A FORCE TO BE RECKONED WITH

IT'S LEFT TO FAMOUS DETECTIVE'S MOTHER TO FOIL 'ANALYTICAL ENGINE' SWINDLE, SAVING GOVERNMENT THOUSANDS

MEANWHILE SHERLOCK – BELIEVED DEAD – FOUND HIDING IN PANTRY OF VILLA

OWNER BERTRAM ALFREDS UNDER ARREST

When a member of the Holmes family prevented a major crime this morning, it was not the once-great detective Sherlock – or his much-decorated brother Mycroft – but their mother Mrs Agatha Effie Theodora Holmes of Knightsbridge. She saved the day by unmasking the much-vaunted 'Metaphysical Engineer' Mr Bertram Alfreds as a charlatan, saving the government a small fortune. Meanwhile Holmes and his faithful friend Dr John Watson were discovered cowering in a pantry after a series of spills and accidents worthy of a music-hall comedy act. Prime Minister Lord Rosebery welcomed the news that Sherlock had amazingly survived his encounter at the Reichenbach Falls three years ago but regretted the apparent decline in the detective's powers. He thanked Mrs Holmes personally, praising her great powers of... (Continued on page 3.)

MACHINE PRINTS BERNOULLI NUMBERS

In the aftermath of the unmasking and arrest of Mr Bertram Alfreds (described left), notable Indian mathematician Mr Sudhakara Dvivedi demonstrated that the Analytical Engine on the premises – built by Alfreds from the plans of Mr Charles Babbage – was printing the mathematically important Bernoulli numbers. Dvivedi said, "I was able to make various improvements to the machine on the basis of notes left by Countess Ada Lovelace and found they worked and the machine delivered the Bernoulli numbers, which is a major development for mathematicians." He added, "It is good to see the Engine returned to its mathematical purpose. It was utterly wasted as a prop in Mr Alfreds' fanciful plot." *The Gazette* understands that Mr Dvivedi has been invited to luncheon at Downing Street.

COACHMAN SOUGHT

Mrs Holmes applauded the help provided by a mysterious handsome coachman, who provided key elements of information to enable her to crack the plot. However, *The Gazette* has found no trace of any handsome coachman on the streets of London this day in April 1894.

PROGRESS IN PARK LANE MURDER

Inspector Lestrade of Scotland Yard announced the arrest of Colonel Sebastian Moran as the murderer of the Honourable Ronald Adair on March 30 in the famous Park Lane Mystery. The Inspector paid tribute to an anonymous helper and also thanked Dr John Watson, former associate of Sherlock Holmes.

UP THE TROPHY ROOM STAIRCASE

On the landing you hear a movement upstairs – the creak of a floorboard and something being knocked over.

Watson's eyes widen and he lays a forefinger on his lips. "Mr Babbage," he whispers. "Death could not hold him..."

"More likely, Mr Bertram Alfreds," you say, "or whoever is working on his behalf, leading us through this succession of puzzles and clues... It looks as though they are getting sloppy."

Watson sets off on tiptoe up the stairs, as if bound for a séance. You follow.

What *has* happened to Watson's usual scientific outlook? He does seem rather fixated on this Babbage fellow. If he were not in your way you would quicken your stride to catch whoever made the noise, but there is no way past the tremulous doctor and you emerge on a small landing behind him.

He is looking at another door. This one has a contraption on it that looks like a lock.

There is a grid of symbols and one empty space. Around the grid you see various equals signs and numbers. On the floor, lie four solid shapes: an arrowhead, a triangle, a pentagon and a square.

"Each symbol represents a number?" Watson asks.

"Correct," you nod. "And the numbers by each column and row tell us what all the symbols in that row or column add up to."

"Let's be swift, Holmes," Watson says, rifling through the shapes. "Babbage isn't confined by our earthly constraints, and we really must catch up to him!"

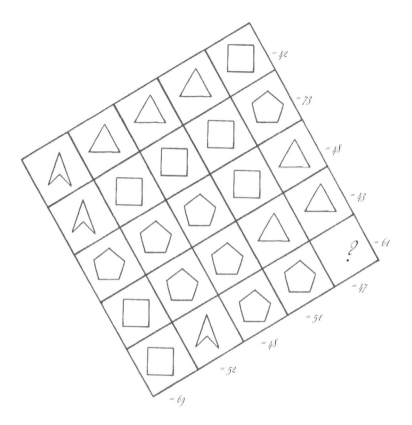

This is getting beyond a joke, you think. "As I said yesterday, work is the best antidote to sorrow, Watson. Let's solve the puzzle at hand."

▶ *Turn to the number you discover*

TIME FOR TEA

On a low table beside the fire you find nine teacups, laid out in a neat square.

Just below the teacups is a message, which appears to be written in tea leaves and sugar. You read it aloud: "What is the smallest number of teacups you need to move to change this shape from a square to a triangle?"

You walk around the table. Watson follows. The teacups move in your mind, configuring triangle after triangle after triangle, then they stop.

Your hand reaches out to move the first cup.

▶ *Turn to the number you discover*

THE ANALYTICAL ENGINE

from 49, 78, 103, 105

You emerge into a cavernous room filled with a large metal contraption.

"This must be...?" Watson turns to you.

"Indeed," you reply, pointing to the engraved name and initials. "Bertram Alfreds." You notice a compass scratched into the front of the machine.

"It is most likely the source of the noise Mrs H. heard," Watson murmurs.

This is not the Engine of Babbage's sketches but another beast entirely, you think.

"Whatever it is doing," you say, "we need to find some way to turn it off."

Watson is holding a handwritten note with a smudge in the corner. "This can't be from Alfreds... Perhaps someone is trying to aid us?"

"Impossible to know," you respond, "but it is the only instruction we have."

> To shut down:
> Combine the levers to determine the way,
> One disc for each step.
> To select the punched card to enter,
> Count with B.A. to find what is missing.

▶ *Walk four steps north and insert a punched card with ten holes – Turn to 103*

▶ *Walk 11 steps north-west and insert a punched card with five holes – Turn to 59*

▶ *Walk to the north of the machine and insert five punched cards – Turn to 49*

HiNts

aNd

SOLutIoNS

221A – HINTS

(2) Library

Consider the missing letters from each book title. What instruction do you see? You may have to do a little unscrambling first.

(3) Engraved Box

Take each statement and consider the implications of that statement being true. Does that statement being true make any other statement true, too?

(6) Carriage 417

The coachman tells you two important pieces of information here:
1. "Watch out for the toolbox!"
2. Ada Lovelace and Charles Babbage used letters to refer to lines of an algorithm, where A = first line, B = second line, etc.

They might be worth remembering.

(10) Main Drawing Room

What else in the room has a similar shape to the cake? How might you be able to manipulate it? Be quick! You're running out of time!

(16) Tile 16

What might you be able to spin to turn these numbers into a direction?

(18) Trapdoor

Try making and folding the net yourself – does this show you which cubes are possible and impossible?

(20) Trophy Room

Do the decoded words point you to any particular object in the room?

(21) Looking for a Cab

Look at the three carriage numbers available. Check each number against the two statements. There is only one number for which both statements are true. Which is it?

(26) **Dining Room**

The scrawled note asks, 'For a man of letters... What colour do you prefer?'
There are a number of highlighted letters. How could you convert these
letters to colours? Do you have a tool at your disposal to do this?

(29) **Attic Windowsill**

Look at the tiles and consider each set as a number in a sequence. What
changes as you move from number to number? Is something added or
removed? Or is there some rule to describe how the pattern grows?
Once you've found it, consider what is additional – this is the tile you'll
need to remove.

(31) **Hall**

The suit of armour's limbs have been contorted to give you a clue. Consider
the left and right hands and feet, and gather the letters in sequence. Think of
the Flying Scotchman. What kind of means of transport is it? That gives you
your first letter.

(41) **Billiard Room**

Consider the different elements in each triangle and how these change as
you move from triangle 1 to triangle 3. What might that mean for what must
come next?

(43) **(Ariadne in the) Linen Cupboard**

Instead of travelling from the outside in, can you travel from the inside out?

(47) **Five-pointed Leaves**

The algorithm here gives you some important information, which might be
worth remembering.

(50) **Attic Bedroom**

A gold cross, a chunk of bread, a glass of wine... where might these objects
commune (-ion)?

(55) The Fifth Book on the Fifth Shelf in the Fifth Bookcase

The algorithm here gives you some important information. It might be worth remembering.

(61) Stay and Investigate

Follow the arrow. What could it be telling you to turn?

(64) Alfreds' Bedroom

When you can't solve a problem, it can often be useful to take a good look at your reflection.

(66) Library Window

It's curious how the four panes of the window seem to demarcate the four parts of the arrangement... Watch for the line of symmetry across the middle, and what that means for any plants that sit directly on it.

(68) "The Language of the Silver Sun"

Perhaps the Code Wheel can be a help here?

(72) A Small Black Box

Consider the letter sent to 221B. There are a number of bold letters – where do they lead you?

(75) An Unveiling

The destination is four letters long.

(79) In the Study

Look at the three completed number triangles. Might the outside numbers work as a team to make the number in the middle? What's important in a team is that some things add, while others are notable for what they take away.

(80) **Inside the Machine**
Consider the muddy fingerprints you've seen over the course of the night.
What might the bird, the cog and the die be referring to? And how might
each relate to the letters 'A', 'D' and 'A'? Think about who else had muddy
fingers, too... Did they say anything that could help?

(81) **Conservatory**
Watson is counting on you to get this right.

(93) **'Z'**
Can you use the Morse code alphabet to decode the message carved into
the banisters?

(98) **In the Garden**
Go through the letter's instructions one by one. For the 'O', look at the
exterior of the house. Can you see anything – natural or man-made – that
could be an 'O'? Use the number of water lilies to count down from there.

(100) **A View of the Ballroom**
Small squares can also be part of large squares – and never forget that the
frame you look through is always a part of the picture.

(101) **Attic Bible**
By viewing each set of numbers as directions to find a specific word,
consider what you would specify to identify any single word on the page.
How might this indicate to you what the numbers are? Can you use the
single word given to help you find the others?

(102) "No Time for Tea"

The paragraph in the book holds all the clues you need to work out where to go next. Start with the word that stands out and then consider the lines below that give you some instructions on how to change it. What could 'No time for tea, Cut it...' mean? And what might 'Instead put YOU, Holding its place, keep it informal' be telling you to do? If you feel unsure or stuck, don't forget to 'Engage with the initials'.

(107) Up the Trophy Room Staircase

You may want to work out what amount each symbol is worth to identify which one fits into the gap. Perhaps rows and columns where there are only a few symbols are good places to start?

(108) Time for Tea

If you consider the top of the triangle to be a single teacup, can you see how many teacups you'd need in the line below, and then again in the line below that?

(109) The Analytical Engine

Look closely at the Engine ahead. With some counting and close observation you should be able to find all the information you need. Look at the compass – what direction is each lever pointing in, and what happens if you combine them? How many discs are there? And how big is Bertram Alfreds' ego?

221B – SOLUTIONS

(2) **Library**
The missing letters are: L (*Paradise Lost*), O (*Oedipus Rex*), O (*On Liberty*), K (*Kidnapped*), O (*Bleak House*), U (*Beowulf*), T (*Vanity Fair*), S (*Frankenstein*), I (*Wuthering Heights*), D (*Tess of the D'Ubervilles*), and E (*Jane Eyre*).

You need to cross to the window to 'Look outside'.

(3) **Engraved Box**
The one true statement is: 'The right button to push is one of 28 and 96', as it is the only statement whose truth is consistent with the other three statements being false.

The second statement being true makes 'Don't push 96' false, so '96' is the correct button to press.

(10) **Main Drawing Room**
Other than the teacups and saucers the only other round item in the room is the face of the grandfather clock.

You can recreate the shape by moving the hands of the grandfather clock to quarter to 12, with the gap between the two hands representing the large slice of cake that has been removed.

(16) **Tile 16**
Using the Code Wheel to decode the list of numbers, you get the following letters: B, E, D, R, O, O, M.

The Bedroom is Room 4.

(18) **Trapdoor**
When formed into a cube, the net creates Cube 56.

(20) Trophy Room

The symbols decode to 'BANG BANG'.

You need to look at the gun case.

(21) Looking for a Cab

The correct answer is 417, as the gap between 4 and 1 is 3, and the two odd numbers, 1 and 7, are next to each other.

(22) Inside the Safe

The decoded message reads: 'BASK IN THE LIGHT OF THE SILVER SUN'.

(26) Dining Room

The bold letters in the tasting notes all code to GREEN on the Code Wheel.

The green door is the correct choice.

(29) Attic Windowsill

There are a number of different ways to think of this sequence of tiles.

One approach is to see that as you move from Pattern 1 to Pattern 2, two tiles are added to the right-hand side of the pattern; as you move from Pattern 2 to Pattern 3, three tiles are added; and so on. The tiles added are indicated in pink below.

Following this pattern, both Tile 73 and Tile 42 are part of the new addition of four tiles, so Tile 16 is the 'additional tile' and should be removed.

(31) Hall

The suit of armour's left hand is pointing to a picture of a train. Its right hand is pointing to rhubarb on the table. The right foot is pointing to an apple. By its left foot is a pear. The first letters of these words spell TRAP.

The trapdoor is the correct choice.

(41) Billiard Room

Consider the four chalked triangles as a sequence. There are five different elements to consider: each square has one ball of each colour; the number of squares visible increases by one as we move through the sequence; while the number of stripes decreases by one; the written numbers increase by one as we move through the sequence, and the letters of the alphabet move backwards by one place.

Considering the contents of Triangle 3 tells us that Triangle 4 needs to include: one ball of each colour, four squares, one stripe, the number 20 and the letter K. Currently missing from Triangle 4 is: a blue ball, one stripe and the number 20.

The '20' blue ball is the correct answer.

(43) (Ariadne in the) Linen Cupboard

The correct answer is 'Z'.

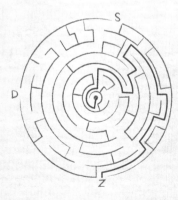

(50) Attic Bedroom

The three objects – the cross, the wine and the bread – all have connections to Christianity, suggesting you should look at the Bible.

(61) Stay and Investigate

Set the Code Wheel to the symbol given. Follow the time shown on the clock and the arrow to turn the Wheel three spaces in a clockwise direction. This will reveal the number 22.

(63) A Floor Plan

The decoded message reads: 'THE ORDER'S LODGE'.

(64) Alfreds' Bedroom

The message needs to be held up to a mirror to be read.
It gives this instruction:

'Take the wheel.
Start at the letter U.
Turn seven places anticlockwise.
Use the number given.'

If you follow these instructions, the Code Wheel will reveal the number 8.

(66) Library Window

There are five plants missing – one at the top and one at the bottom, one on the left and two on the right. Note that the cross of the window represents two lines of symmetry. There are six plants that sit on the lines of symmetry.

(68) "The Language of the Silver Sun"

The decoded message reads: 'FOR THOSE WHO DARE... TO THE UNDERWORLD. GO TO THE BASEMENT.'

(72) **A Small Black Box**

The bold letters in Bertram's letter tell you to 'Turn to sixty eight', indicating you should turn to entry 68.

(75) **An Unveiling**

You should find the word 'Hall' in the jumbled letters.
Using the floor plan you can see that the Hall is Room 31.

(79) **In the Study**

The pattern is as follows: the bottom-left number is subtracted from the top number, then the bottom-right number is subtracted from the top number. These two numbers are then added together.

Therefore, to find the missing number, you need to complete the following sums: 16 - 2 = 14
16 - 13 = 3
14 + 3 = 17

80 **Inside the Machine**

You've been given three mysterious algorithms on your journey through the house, all supposedly written by Ada Lovelace. Ada's name on the wall, along with the three symbols, suggests that now is the moment to use them.

The small symbols are indicating you should use Ada's bird algorithm first, her engine algorithm second, and the gambling algorithm third. These were on the three pieces of paper Irene Adler, in her disguise as the gardener, left for you, all marked with her muddy fingerprints.

The letters 'A', 'D' and 'A' in Ada's name are also telling you which line to use from each algorithm. If you remember, the coachman (also Irene Adler in disguise) informed you that this was a technique used by Babbage and Lovelace, where letters of the alphabet were used to refer to particular lines.

You need to use line one from the bird algorithm, line four from the engine algorithm, and line one from the gambling algorithm. These give you the following instructions for the Code Wheel:

1. Take the Wheel, start at 'B'
2. Turn it 10 places anticlockwise
3. Take the number given and turn the Wheel clockwise by this number.

The colour shown is BLUE, indicating you should turn the blue handle.

81 **Conservatory**

'Pent up' suggests the Greek *penta* (five). 'E' is the fifth letter of the alphabet. There are five senses and five vowels. The clues all point you to the number five, sending you to the plant with the five-pointed leaves.

93 **'Z'**

Using the Morse code alphabet, the decoded message reads: 'GO LEFT'.

(98) In the Garden

The goddess statue is pointing to the left, so you need to look at the right side of the house.

The 'O' is made out of ivy and is around the top-right window.

There are two lilies in the pond.

If you count two down from the top right-hand window you'll find that the correct window is in the bottom right-hand corner.

(100) A View of the Ballroom

There are five squares in the window frame that you are looking through (four smaller panels and one full window frame).

There are 22 squares within the windows you can see in the Ballroom (16 small squares – eight per window – then three larger squares in each window).

There are ten squares on the floor (two large ones and eight smaller ones at the corners).

There are 37 squares in total.

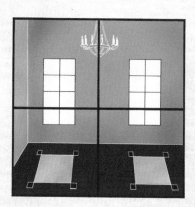

(101) Attic Bible

Each set of three numbers refers to a single word on the page.

The first number indicates the paragraph, and then the second two (within the brackets), tell you the line and the word on that line.

So, '8 (1,1)' indicates the eighth paragraph and then tells you to look for the first word in the first line, which is 'He'.

Using this method to pull words from text, the following message will be revealed: 'He made an engine. It will cause terror. Make it be no more.'

(102) "No Time for Tea"

Start by taking the word 'steady'.

The instructions tell you: 'No time for tea, cut it', so you need to remove the word 'tea'. This gives you 's___dy'.

Then, you are told 'and instead put YOU, Holding its place, keep it informal'. 'Holding its place' suggests that 'YOU' should replace 'tea'. Informal indicates what type of 'you' to use.

The final clue is 'Engage with the initials'. The first letter of the first word in each line spells 'FRENCH'. This is indicating that you should insert the informal 'you' in French, which is 'tu'.

The correct answer is 'study'.

107 **Up the Trophy Room Staircase**
The shapes have the following values:
Square = 17
Triangle = 4
Pentagon = 9
Arrowhead = 13

The missing shape is the arrowhead.

108 **Time for Tea**
You need to move two teacups to change the shape from a square to
a triangle.

(109) **The Analytical Engine**
Using the compass on the side of the machine, you can see that the two
levers are pointing north and west. If you combine these you get the
direction north-west.

There are 11 discs on the machine – four at the very front, and then an
additional seven down the side – so you need to take 11 steps.

Bertram has written his initials 'B.A.' a total of five times on the Engine.
This number tells you that you want a punched card with five holes.

Putting this together, Holmes and Watson must face north-west, take
11 steps and put a punched card with five holes into the machine.

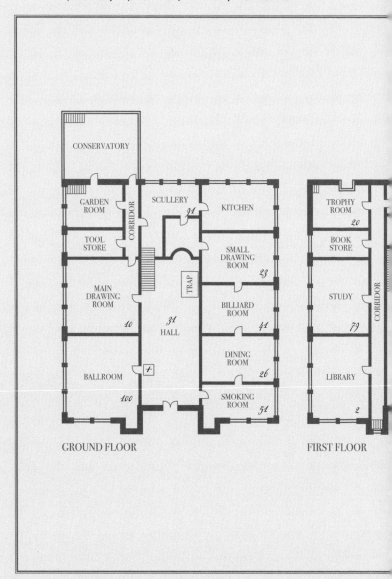

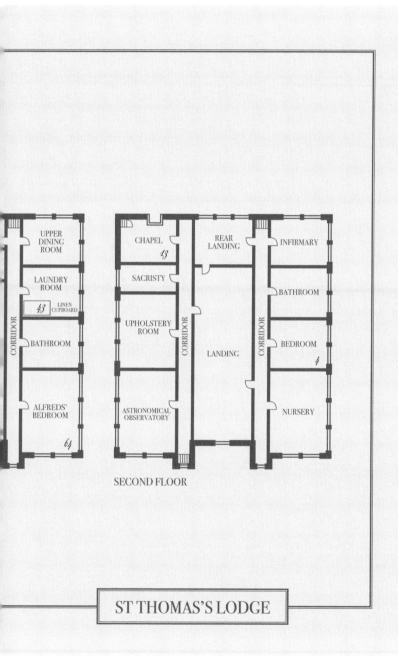

UPPER DINING ROOM

LAUNDRY ROOM

43 LINEN CUPBOARD

BATHROOM

ALFREDS' BEDROOM

64

CORRIDOR

CHAPEL

13

SACRISTY

UPHOLSTERY ROOM

ASTRONOMICAL OBSERVATORY

CORRIDOR

REAR LANDING

LANDING

CORRIDOR

INFIRMARY

BATHROOM

BEDROOM

4

NURSERY

SECOND FLOOR

ST THOMAS'S LODGE

FLOOR PLAN

First published 2022 by
Ammonite Press
an imprint of Guild of Master Craftsman Publications Ltd
Castle Place, 166 High Street, Lewes, East Sussex, BN7 1XU,
United Kingdom

Reprinted 2022, 2023

ISBN 978-1-78145-441-1

A catalogue record for this book is available from the British Library.

Publisher: Jonathan Bailey
Designer: Robin Shields
Editor: Laura Paton
Additional Text: Viv Croot

Colour reproduction by GMC Reprographics
Printed and bound in China

If you've escaped the pages (or are still trapped!) please
send us a message: **#SherlockHolmesEscapeBook**
@ammonitepress

AMMONITE
PRESS

www.ammonitepress.com